# SKETCH *to* SIX+ FIGURES

# SKETCH *to* SIX+ FIGURES

HOW TO BUILD A PROFITABLE BUSINESS
WITH COURAGE & CREATIVITY

## MARY AGHEDO

First Edition, 2025

ISBN: 979-899-89060-1-5 (Hardback)
979-899-89060-2-2 (Paperback)
979-899-89060-3-9 (Ebook)

Published by Dezua Events Limited
www.dezua.com
info@dezua.com

Editor: Joy Ehonwa and Stacey Kay
Editorial Support: Nadine Onaiwu
Author's Photo: Sarah Wells
Cover and Layout Design: Adebayo Gbenga

# Praise For *Sketch to Six+ Figures*

"This book is timely and powerful. It teaches people how to take their business from zero to one hundred, how to build from scratch and grow step by step into giants in their industries. I believe it carries lessons not just for Nigeria, but for Africa as a whole.

Above all, it reflects grit, guts, resilience and the kind of tenacity it takes to bring real value to the table."
**—Funke Bucknor, Founder & CEO, Zapphaire Events**

"Taking us through her story, we get a roadmap for every creative to navigate the highs and lows of starting and growing a business. This book is honest, witty and hard to put down. From the very first page, you are drawn into Mary's world, which could easily be your world.

This is not just a book, it's a manual and a must-have for every creative. It's a reminder that you are not alone, and a testament that if you have faith and refuse to let society define success for you, you can achieve success on your terms. This is a great addition to anyone's library."
**—Rev. Lanre Oluseye, South-South Regional Director, House On The Rock**

"I've seen Mary's creativity up close. She handled my wedding décor so beautifully and with such heart that it left a lasting impression. That same excellence and intentionality shine through in *Sketch to Six+ Figures*.

Reading the book felt like sitting across from her as she generously shared the wisdom, experiences and principles that shaped her journey. What I appreciate most is how practical it is; beyond the inspiration, the steps she outlines are clear and actionable.

It's a refreshing and encouraging read, a reminder that with vision, consistency and the right mindset, growth and success are truly attainable."

**—Mercy Chinwo Blessed, Award-Winning Gospel Music Artist**

"Mary Aghedo's *Sketch to Six+ Figures* is a masterclass in entrepreneurial courage and creativity. The author poignantly captures the struggles many creatives face: being overwhelmed by business responsibilities, lacking mentorship and navigating uncertainty. Yet, Mary's story offers hope and inspiration.

Her storytelling approach makes complex business concepts accessible and inspiring. Her journey from chaos to building a lasting brand is a testament to perseverance and adaptability.

The book's message is clear: with determination and creativity, even the most ambitious ideas can become profitable, purpose-built realities.

A must-read for creatives, entrepreneurs and anyone looking to build a sustainable business"

**—Hon. Marilyn Okowa-Daramola, Member, Delta State House of Assembly**

"*Sketch to Six+ Figures* is a practical guide to help creatives turn their passion into a profitable business. Through personal storytelling, Mary shares courageous, real-world decisions and actionable strategies that enable creatives to monetise their craft without compromising their voice.

A concise, inspiring roadmap for growing a creative practice with integrity and impact."
**—Tareela Okene, Founder & CEO, Dripples Cakes**

"From designing on drawing boards to calculating at offshore rigs, from collecting wedding magazines that fill up a room to building an empire we all know as Dezua Events, her journey has been extraordinary.

Mary never gave up on herself or her dreams, even when no one was clapping, and today she is a force to be reckoned with.

This book lets you see through Mary's eyes and gives you the drive to keep going, as a creative, designer, curator or dreamer, because the glory is in the journey."
**—Munachi Abii, Award-Winning Actress & Filmmaker**

# Table of Contents

# *Dedication*



To every creative bold enough to build on their gift.
This book is for you.

# Introduction

The downfall of many gifted creatives is hardly a lack of talent. It's operating in chaos for too long.

It usually starts with magic: a spark of brilliance, a few wins, and glowing compliments. Your eye is unmatched. Your ideas? Unforgettable. But soon, the cracks begin to show. Missed details. Late nights. Disorganised folders. Endless voice notes. You're doing great work, but behind the scenes, it's barely holding together.

You've become the entire business: the project lead, the logistics officer, the admin, the client's therapist. You're praised for your gift but pulled apart by everything else it takes to keep going.

*Sketch to Six+ Figures* is here to help you fix that, before chaos becomes your normal.

This book is part memoir, part guide. It's written for creatives like you: the ones who started with talent, not templates. The ones who can deliver their craft flawlessly but freeze when it's time to price it. The ones doing everything right on the outside but quietly wondering how much longer they can keep going like this.

I've been there. I built from scratch with no roadmap and no clear formula, just a deep conviction that my gift deserved more than survival. What started as a sketch evolved into a profitable, purpose-built business that now operates with clarity, structure and intention.

And while it looks polished now, there were moments I considered quitting, not because I stopped loving the work, but because the weight of managing everything made it hard to breathe.

Here's what you'll get inside:

- Strategies for overcoming fear and self-doubt
- Mindset and confidence shifts
- Ways to set early boundaries and protect your brand value
- Lessons on systems and profitability
- Team and leadership growth principles
- Strategies for scaling wisely, securing wealth and crafting a meaningful legacy
- Access to practical tools for budgeting

If you've ever said, 'I just want to do the work I love', this book will show you how to do exactly that, without losing your mind or your margins. Because the goal isn't only to stay booked. It's to build something that runs with grace, grows with focus, and lasts without burning you out.

Here's what I know for sure: Creativity may open doors, but only systems keep the lights on.

So read this book now. Not after the next client complaint. Not when you finally have 'time'. Now, while your gift is still potent and your business is still malleable.

Let's build what chaos can't break.

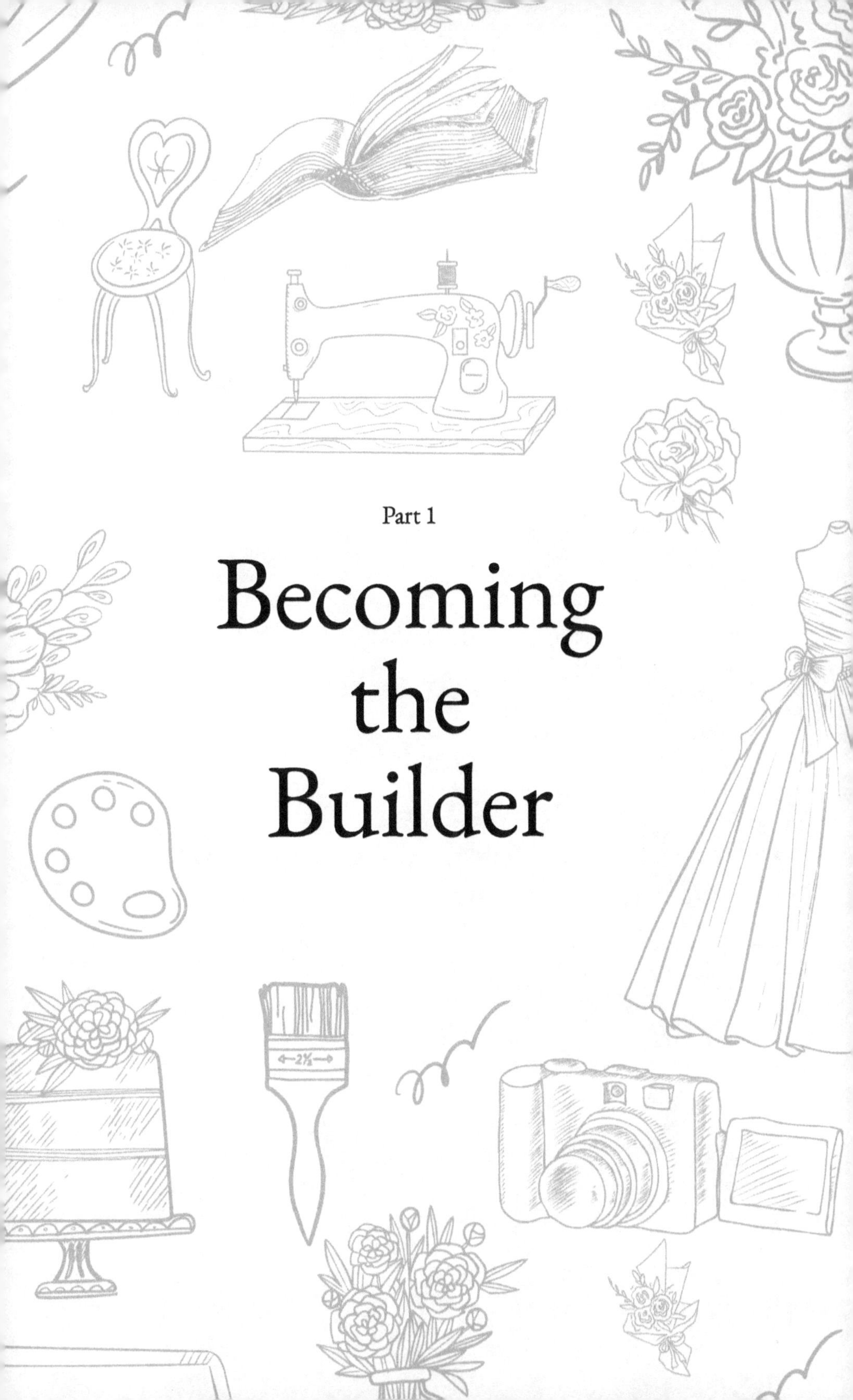



# Becoming the Builder

# Chapter 1

# *A Sketchy First Step*

**Naming it**

'I've figured it out! I've got it! Dezua Events!'

Crickets . . .

I had burst into the living room like I'd just cracked a decades-old code. My heart was racing. It felt like I had named something sacred. I was sure my flatmate would feel the moment too.

But Amaka didn't even look up from her phone. Not even a 'hmm'.

It stung a little, I won't lie. But to be fair, she'd endured six long weeks of me turning our shared flat into what she jokingly called 'a shrine'. Drapes thrown over chairs, centrepieces lined up by the wall, candles, ribbons and runners everywhere, all in the name of training. Our living room became part classroom, part rehearsal space—and I was the only student.

Towards the end of those weeks, I became obsessed with one thing: finding a name. Not just any name. *The* name. Something that would look good on a business card, command respect on an invoice and carry the weight of the vision I was building. I wanted a name with elegance. Intention. Something completely mine. Something that could grow with me.

And I struggled.

I played around with trendy names. Elegant ones. Abstract ones. But nothing stuck. Then I found myself circling back to something familiar. Adesuwa. My middle name. It means 'born into wealth' in Edo.

For me, it meant potential: born with the ability to build wealth or create something valuable with my hands, my ideas, my work.

I initially considered Dessy Events—short, sweet, safe. But then it happened. A moment of clarity. A name that had been waiting patiently to be remembered.

Dezua.

It was bold. Rhythmic. Rooted. It sounded like me, but also like a brand that could outgrow me. It felt like a future I wasn't yet ready for, but one I could grow into. Even if Amaka didn't jump up in excitement (I couldn't blame her; she'd watched me arrange the same set of vases in five different ways), I knew I had found it.

That was the day Dezua Events was born. And quietly, in a small flat with props on the floor and dreams in my chest, something big had begun.

That's the funny thing about beginnings. They rarely come with background music or a lightning bolt. Just you, in your slippers, naming something that no one else believes in yet. And hoping you're not being ridiculous.

I wish I could say I felt sure—that after naming Dezua, I felt like a CEO in the making. What I actually felt was . . . exposed. Like I'd made a promise I had no clue how to keep. There were no clients knocking, and there was no money coming in, but I had done the hardest thing already: I had started. Even if no one cheered me on. Even if it looked like a phase. Even if I had to carry the weight of the name alone for a while.

There's power in simply starting. It appears the moment you decide to stop waiting for readiness and take the first step.

I named it. I claimed it. And readiness? It showed up eventually.

**Recognising Early Cues**

Think about this: What if your gift has been showing up all along, but in ways too subtle to count as 'serious'?

Maybe you thought it was just a quirk, a habit: That thing you always notice. The way you line things up, colour coordinate your clothes, rearrange furniture when no one asked or obsess over details that others don't even see. Maybe you've brushed it off as 'being extra' or 'being particular'. But what if these patterns have always been pointing somewhere?

That's how mine showed up.

There was no grand unveiling. Creativity didn't walk into my life and announce, 'This is who you are now'. It was always there, quietly, in how I moved through the world and the way I couldn't help but make things feel right.

I used to arrange my desk like a tiny showroom. Match my notebooks to my teacup. Style the dining table in ways that upstaged the meal. I was always that child who brought out the Christmas tree every year and decorated the house for the holiday in matching colours and homemade themes. I needed things to feel coordinated, balanced and beautiful. My niece once called me the Queen of To-Match. I laughed, but I didn't argue. She was right.

It wasn't about matching colours alone. I liked flow. Order. Details. In secondary school, while most people loved subjects like economics or biology, I was drawn to technical drawing. Give me a T-square and clean paper, and I was happy. There was joy in straight lines. Proportions. Balance. I didn't realise it was a gift. I thought I was weirdly obsessed with shapes.

I went on to study engineering because it seemed like a good fit at the time. It was respectable. A 'professional course' my family could be proud of. But even then, the signs were there. I couldn't change the way I saw things.

While preparing for presentations, my classmates focused on graphs, formulas and all the important stuff. I, on the other hand, would spend so much time adjusting margins, beautifying charts and choosing colour palettes for slides no one else cared about, because it mattered to me.

At the time, I didn't call it *creativity*. I called it *overdoing*. And I definitely didn't see a career in it. However, I now realise that your gift may not show up in the way you imagine. It might arrive as subtle clues you've been overlooking. In how you arrange. In how you obsess. In how you perceive.

There's something powerful about the patterns you don't remember learning. The things you do without trying. The moments where your brain says, 'Wait, let's make this better', even when no one else sees a problem.

If you look back, you might find that your own trail has been forming too. Maybe you were the one organising the class party. Or redoing your friends' CVs because you couldn't stand the fonts. Maybe you always spotted the one off-note in a song, or the crooked frame in a room, or an uneven seam in an outfit, or the way a photo could've been better if the subject was moved half an inch to the left. These are not accidents. They're echoes of creativity.

So, here's what I want you to do: Look again. At the things you've always done naturally. The parts of you that felt strange, extra or hard to explain. Those could be hints. And when you start treating them like signals instead of noise, you start to uncover the gifts they've been pointing to all along.

**It Was Messy, but It Was Mine**
They say start small. What they don't say is how small.

They don't tell you that your first 'team' might be your sister, two loyal friends and a handful of freelancers you barely know. They don't mention that you'll likely spend more than you make. And they definitely don't tell you that after pulling off the most difficult event of your life, another event designer might stroll in, take photos and pass off your work as hers. Yep! That happened.

No one really warns you about that part.

I didn't ease into the industry with a soft launch or a polished portfolio. I started with a 600-guest setup, no staff and no inventory, standing in the middle of Civic Centre—at the time the largest and most unforgiving event centre in the city of Port Harcourt—wondering if I'd just made the most expensive mistake of my life.

You want to talk about messy? I was unbranded, under-resourced and in way over my head. But somehow, what emerged from that unstructured setup was something that looked nothing like my budget but exactly like my vision. And in that moment, standing in a space I had no business transforming, I realised something that still shapes how I build: It takes one decision to get started.

I'd poured all my savings and the entire client payment into buying materials from scratch. There was no fallback plan. Just me and my small team who stayed up through the night, draping fabrics, arranging chairs and helping me breathe through the anxiety.

We didn't sleep. We set up through sheer willpower. I tied bows with shaking hands and mentally rehearsed how to explain to the client if it all fell apart. I didn't have the language for my design style yet. What I had was instinct. But when I stepped back, exhausted and slightly stunned, I saw something bold and beautiful staring back at me.

By morning, word spread around the city. Other event designers came by to see what the young newcomer had done. One of them even brought a photographer. I didn't think much of it at the time. I was flattered, to be honest. Until I realised the photos weren't for admiration. They were for marketing. Not mine—hers. She eventually used them to brand her bus.

When I finally tried to show people what I had created, I kept hearing the same thing: 'Oh, I know the person who did that'. Except . . . they didn't. It was hard to prove it was mine, especially as an unknown designer with only phone pictures as evidence. But that didn't change the truth. That was my design. That was my setup. That was my start.

And, no, I didn't walk away from that job with profit or clients or any kind of real recognition. What I had was a bruised thumb and the slow realisation that someone else was taking credit for work I had lost sleep—and nearly sanity—over.

But I also had something else: a beginning.

The kind that leaves you sore and half delirious, yet certain that against all odds, you pulled it off.

It was messy, bold and exhausting. But it was mine.

## Still Figuring It Out

What happens when your first big moment doesn't lead to your next one?

There's a stretch of time between discovering your gift and becoming confident in it. It's not quite a start, and it's definitely not the peak. It's that awkward, in-between season where you're still unsure if what you love can become what you do. That's where I found myself right after my first event.

I had launched. I had proof that it could work. But I didn't yet know what 'working' would actually look like. I didn't have a blueprint or mentors around me doing what I hoped to do. I wasn't even sure what to charge, or if I'd get another job soon. I had more questions than understanding, but I also had momentum. And for where I was at that stage, that was enough.

I did what I could with what I had. I kept building slowly. I studied the designs of professionals I admired to understand balance and flow. I went back to sketching, explored materials, paid attention to finishing.

I wasn't waiting for someone to give me permission. I was preparing.

Because I had chosen to treat this like a real business from the beginning, I held myself to a standard. I didn't want to be seen as 'just a decorator'. I wanted to be known as a creative director, someone with process, presence and results. So, I kept showing up with that mindset, even when I felt unsure behind the scenes.

That shift made all the difference. It changed how I spoke about my work. It shaped how I documented each event. It gave me the patience to build something lasting.

There's no perfect formula for that stage. But if you're in it, I want you to know that the discomfort you feel means you're stepping into something real.

Keep moving; the path reveals itself as you walk.

## No Blueprint? No Problem

Let's be honest: how prepared can you be?

How prepared can you really be for your first real client? Or your first 'can you give us a proposal' email? How ready can you truly feel the first time someone says yes to a job you weren't even sure how to price?

People talk about being prepared like it's a finish line. But if you're doing something new, really new, there is no such thing. You don't prepare your way into experience. You act your way into it.

When I started, I didn't have systems in place. What I had were scribbles on paper, too many Google searches and a high tolerance for late nights. I designed before I had templates. I charged before I understood profit. I barely knew how to make mood boards. I had ideas I'd gathered from everywhere, hoping they made sense together. And sometimes . . . I guessed. I moved because waiting wasn't building anything.

I made daring promises that could have gone terribly wrong, like the time I committed to a floral ceiling installation before checking if the ceiling could hold it. It was my idea: a floating floral canopy across the entire tent. The kind of design that makes clients gasp. I sold it like I had done it ten times. In truth, I had no clue what the ceiling framework was made of. No confirmed rigging plan or structural drawing. What I had was great enthusiasm and a suspicious amount of confidence.

At around 2:00 a.m. the night before the setup, I was hunched over the dining table with one eye closed, sketching a new support system. I was sore all over from all the preparations. My only backup plan? Pray the venue manager wouldn't ask too many questions.

Somehow, we pulled it off. The florals 'floated'. The client beamed. And I made a mental note: Next time, please check the ceiling before you try to hang the sky.

That was the rhythm of my early days. There was no blueprint, but I was building one with every yes, every pivot, every problem I had to solve at the eleventh hour.

Some people wait until they have a mapped-out process. I took action because I didn't have the luxury of delay. By the time I figured out one thing, two more jobs had come in—ready or not. And that's what sharpened me.

I was learning judgement. Learning what to ask, what to quote, what to avoid, what to double-check and, most of all, how to bounce back from mistakes.

Sometimes, the mistakes were costly. Like the time I forgot to include stage design in the budget. The priciest element of my design, I just left it out entirely. On my way home, I remembered, and panic hit. I couldn't go back to retrieve the budget, so I ended up completing the project at a loss. The next time I priced an event, stage design was the very first line item—and it still is to this day.

I didn't figure out how to quote better from a perfect business plan; I figured it out by doing and by moving forward. Plans are great, but momentum? Momentum will teach you what planning can't. That's how most builders learn.

So, if you're stuck at the start line, waiting for more insights, know this: that feeling of 'readiness' may not come. Start anyway.

You'll improvise. You'll forget things. You'll build midair. But then, you'll discover what you're made of. That's what builders do: We don't wait for certainty. We make progress and let clarity catch up.

No blueprint? No problem. Keep building forward.

## Start Brave, Not Big

There was a time when every prop I owned could fit into a corner of my father's garage. Not a warehouse. Not a studio. Just one corner, wedged between an old car and a stack of paint buckets that no one wanted to throw away. That was the headquarters of Dezua. And yet, I recall someone referring to it as 'a design company'. Not a hustle. Not 'your side business'. A company.

They said it casually, probably didn't even think twice about it. But I did. Deep down, I knew they weren't wrong. What I was building *was* a company. Only it didn't look like one yet.

We often assume confidence must be earned by size—team size, budget size, client size, warehouse size. But confidence isn't a reward. It's a decision.

To start brave is to present your brand with intention, even while you're still figuring things out. It's about showing up fully, before you feel ready. It's saying, 'I built this and it's worth something'—even if what you've built is still scrappy and sitting beside your dad's old tires.

Bravery is what separates builders from people who are testing the waters. And when you start with bravery, you make decisions that protect the future.

I remember turning down a client who wanted luxury on a backyard budget. The job might have boosted my visibility, but I knew that saying yes would mean shrinking, apologising, and justifying my worth for the next six weeks. I would also have set the tone for how I was valued by this client and every subsequent referral.

I questioned my decision, but I stood firm. That single act of bravery made me proud, and that pride began to shape my work, my posture, my pricing and eventually, my brand.

I learned something crucial: how you start matters. Starting small is fine. Starting unsure is expected. But starting passive? That's a choice.

Choose to start brave.

# *Builder's Note*

## The Beginning Stages

Every conceptual journey passes through three powerful phases early on. The key is to recognise them as defining seasons of growth:

1.  **The Spark Stage:** You begin noticing your natural eye for detail or ease with design. It feels instinctive. Inspiration strikes and you feel the first creative pull.

**What to do:** Honour it. Nurture the spark. Your creativity is pointing you somewhere.

2.  **The Shift Stage:** You move from idea to action. You start taking imperfect steps and dealing with self-doubt.

**What to do:** Take it seriously. Start building and package your gift like it matters.

3.  **The Stretch Stage:** You've started. You're doing the work. You're unsure but committed.

**What to do:** Stay consistent. Keep learning and refining. Speak about your work professionally, regardless of your audience size.

## Builder's Tasks:

1.  Write the truth about where you are. Be honest. Garage? Spare room? Laptop and a dream? Put it on paper. That's your starting line.

2.  Decide how you want to be seen at this point. What do you want clients to feel when they find your brand?

3.  Draft one brave message. It could be your bio, your service caption, or your proposal cover. Write something that sounds like the version of you you're building towards.

4.  Say no once, on purpose. Turn down one thing that doesn't align with your values, even if it feels uncomfortable.

5. Raise one small standard. Improve how you send your next quote. Edit your social media profile. Use a clearer name for your folders. Just one thing, but do it like it matters.

# Chapter 2

# *Outgrowing the 9–5 Mindset*

## 9–5 Was the Default Dream

Growing up in Nigeria, we were taught, directly and indirectly, that the surest path to a decent, successful and comfortable life was through a corporate job.

Graduate and get a decent-paying role in a respected organisation. That was the dream. And from as early as secondary school, the system started sorting us towards it.

The 'intelligent' ones were nudged towards professional courses such as medicine, law, engineering and architecture. These were the emblems of brilliance. The proof that you were headed for a great future. Parents would beam with pride as they introduced their children by their professional titles: 'My daughter, the doctor', 'My son, the engineer'. Not necessarily because of what the child loved, but because of what the career signified: security, prestige and proof that the hard work of parenting had paid off.

Business, on the other hand, especially creative business, was considered something different entirely. It was for the 'unserious' or 'less book-smart'. If you were truly bright, you didn't become a decorator or a baker or a fashion designer. That path was for the uneducated, the trophy wives, or those with time to spare and family who could provide.

And for a while, I bought into that belief too.

Even after I had started the business and was doing good work, I struggled to own it. I loved event design, but I felt it was beneath the level of intelligence we had been trained to value. I felt embarrassed to introduce myself as an event designer. I avoided the title and the full truth. It didn't sound intellectual enough. Especially for a woman who had graduated top of her class in a male-dominated faculty.

The society didn't help either. I could hear the polite pause in people's voices when I explained what I did. I noticed how some friends would subtly downplay my work, unintentionally or otherwise. Their 9–5s were positioned as more serious, more structured, more respectable. Sometimes it came with a joke—'So the engineer is now playing with ribbons?'—and we all laughed. But underneath the laughter was the message: This path can't be the real career.

I noticed early enough that people usually don't validate what they don't understand. Your family might not see the vision. Your partner might not know how to support it. Your friends might joke about your new hustle like it's a phase. But that doesn't make your vision any less valid. It just means the vision was given to you, not them.

I remember telling my husband I wanted to go into event design. He smiled and said something like, 'Isn't that what women do when they're bored? You're an engineer. You should be working in an established company'.

We joked about it, but it caught me off guard. It felt like he couldn't quite see the possibility I was trying to explore, like he'd placed my dream in a box labelled 'not serious'. I didn't take it to heart, but in that moment, I realised I might have to walk this path without immediate understanding or validation. And that was okay.

It took years to shed that shame and to accept that the business I was building, the creativity I was stewarding and the courage it took to keep showing up wasn't a downgrade. It was a different kind of brilliance.

## Breaking the 'Only Way' Mentality

Walking into the office for the first time felt surreal.

It was my first 'real' job. There was an actual assignment letter in hand, a desk to my name and a future that looked as promising as they'd always said it would. I had interned with this same company as a student, but this felt different. I was now a graduate engineer. I could potentially be a few months away from heading to the oil rigs. The butterflies were very real.

The first few days were a blur of excitement. I wanted to do everything well. I was motivated, alert and ready to prove myself. But by the second month, the excitement had worn off. The 4:00 a.m. rush to beat Lagos traffic became draining. The rhythm of clocking in and clocking out felt more like a loop than a life. I wasn't burnt out, at least not yet. But I was restless. And I didn't understand why.

This was the job many people dreamed of. It was secure, prestigious and well-paying. Yet, I found myself dragging through the days, forcing energy that didn't feel real anymore. Was I being ungrateful? Lazy? Mentally weak? I started to question myself. After all, this was supposed to be it, the dream. So why didn't it feel like my dream anymore?

I remember pacing around the office well after closing hours one evening, torn between guilt and confusion. Then I picked up my phone and called a friend, someone I had studied with at university.

We exchanged pleasantries, and I tried to keep the conversation casual, but he could tell something was off. That wasn't hard to spot since I had become terrible at keeping in touch due to the demanding job. And here I was repeating variants of the same pleasantries.

He went straight to the point and asked, 'Mary, what's wrong?'

I hesitated. I didn't know how to say what was on my mind. But I needed to speak to someone. Someone whose opinion I respected.

Someone who wouldn't judge me. So I summoned the courage and finally blurted it out.

'Is it okay if I don't want to work for an oil company?'

I felt exposed, ashamed even. Like I was confessing to a failure. I had always imagined this was where I'd thrive. How could I now be questioning everything?

I continued, still unsure:

'Would I be crazy to leave? Will people think me a failure if I try something else?'

He paused for a moment, long enough for me to regret asking these 'silly' questions. But then his response was nothing like I expected. In his usual calm, wise tone, he said something that gave me permission to exhale:

'I think it's okay to follow your heart, Mary'.

Those words made me light up. I could finally feel the weight lift. I began telling him about another idea I had been secretly nurturing. A different path I had been daydreaming about.

He didn't laugh. He didn't judge.

That night, I pulled out the pile of *Ovation* and *The Wedding Planner* magazines I had been saving. On one of the pages was an ad for a training programme in event design. It felt different from the rest. Something about it resonated with me. The next morning, I reached out to the contact on the page. They responded.

And just like that, the building began.

I didn't know it at the time, but that phone call marked the beginning of a new mindset. One where having a good job didn't automatically mean living a fulfilled life. One where I stopped needing the world's definition of success to approve mine. One where 'only way' thinking finally gave way to possibility.

**You Don't Have to Quit to Think Bigger**

My favourite quote by Alex Hormozi is: 'Your 9–5 isn't killing your dreams. Wasting your 5–9 is'.

It says everything, really. Too many people assume the only way to chase their dreams is to quit. To stage a dramatic exit, burn the bridges and declare to the world, 'I'm done with this life'. But legacy-minded thinkers move differently. They recognise that you don't have to kill one career to give another a chance to live. You can expand your vision without blowing up your foundation.

Working a day job doesn't betray your creativity. And you're not betraying your education by choosing something different.

Some of the most remarkable creative businesses started while their owners still had day jobs. They built proposals after hours. Sent invoices on lunch breaks. Prepped for installations over weekends. Because thinking bigger sometimes may just mean smarter time management.

You can take your evenings and invest them in what you're building. Use your weekends to sketch the framework for your future, the early hours before work to design a business that will one day outgrow your salary. Your job can be a stage. It can fund your growth, shape your discipline and still be a stepping stone to something bigger. If you play it right, you can leave from a place of clarity.

Some creative entrepreneurs left when their business structure was strong, clients were consistent and the systems were in place.

I wish I had waited that long. I left, too, but with less clarity, more fear and nothing close to a perfect plan.

**The Pressure and Peace of Ownership**

I got up and I left.

Newly married, with my husband living in a different city, I had the perfect excuse, the kind that made my exit feel reasonable to the 'people watching'. But somewhere inside, it felt cowardly. Questions kept hovering in my head: Is this what I wanted to do with my life now? Gamble my future away on a business idea? Live in a slower-paced city?

Even though I had a plan, had already completed the décor training and was pitching to land my first project, I still panicked. A few weeks after moving, I began job hunting again. I applied endlessly to corporate organisations. Each rejection stung. It was like I had deliberately missed the bus, and it wasn't coming back.

I had started the business, but I still felt incomplete. Like I had walked away from something I hadn't earned the right to leave. And in a way, the real discomfort wasn't about money. It was the absence of a stable job, the thing I'd spent my whole life looking forward to having. Now that it was gone, I didn't know what to do with myself.

I felt my day job took over my life because it meant waking up at 3:00 a.m., getting to the office two hours early in a bid to dodge the infamous Lagos traffic, sleeping in my car until time to resume, reporting in at 7:00 a.m., sitting through meetings that felt like they'd never end, attending to endless deliverables and watching the clock inch slowly towards closing time.

It felt like something to survive. Still, there was comfort in knowing what to expect.

In the corporate world, your responsibilities are assigned. Your job description is clear. People above you decide the pace, the deadlines, the budget. You get paid at the end of the month regardless of the business wins or losses. There's a form of safety in it. You close your laptop and your day ends.

When the business is yours, your day never truly ends. You may close your laptop, but your mind keeps ticking. The pressure doesn't clock out. You think in deliveries, client follow-ups, staff issues, unpaid invoices, upcoming projects and timelines. And even when nothing is going wrong, you still feel the weight of keeping things going.

The truth is, being an owner doesn't give you instant freedom. It gives you full responsibility. You now create the clock. You set the pace for the team. You make the final calls. You carry the vision. That shift is hard to prepare for, especially when you've been trained to become an employee.

But even with all the pressure, I'd still choose this again. Because ownership grows you in a way no job ever can.

## The Illusion of Job Security Still Follows You

Security was the goal.

Back in the day, it was the highest form of success we understood. Get a good job, earn a steady income, avoid poverty. And when you're raised in a society where unemployment is the villain in every cautionary tale, stability becomes a badge of honour. Salary became the safe zone.

Even after we leave that world, the mindset follows us. We crave what feels predictable, looks respectable and pays on time.

We build our businesses. We get a few wins under our belt. Things start to look promising. But the moment momentum slows or payments are delayed, we panic because we've been conditioned to fear unpredictability. We second-guess ourselves, thinking, 'Maybe I should look for something more stable . . . just in case'.

I remember when Dezua was thriving. We had grown our team, moved into a new office space and streamlined our processes. On the outside, everything looked solid. But as soon as bookings slowed down for a month, I found myself spiralling. The panic hit. It was that old fear whispering: what if this isn't sustainable?

It wasn't the financial dip that unsettled me; it was the fear that business was uncertain. That belief that no matter how brilliant the work was, nothing could beat a steady paycheque.

There's nothing wrong with wanting to feel secure. It's human.

But over time, I've learned that job security is an illusion too. Layoffs happen. Companies restructure. Departments disappear. And more importantly, you can outgrow a job long before it outgrows you.

Entrepreneurship is not less secure. It's a different kind of security. You earn from value, not time. You build systems that outlive your hustle.

It takes time to shift your mindset, to stop seeing entrepreneurship as risky and start seeing it as the freedom to own your time, your income and your future. Real security is in ownership. It's in designing a business that doesn't need a perfect economy to stay afloat. It's in knowing that even if one stream slows down, you've built the capacity to create another.

When you step into this realisation, you stop chasing security. You begin to understand that real security is created by people brave enough to build it on their own terms.

# *Builder's Note*

## Rethinking Safety

This chapter is written for creatives who feel themselves shrinking inside a life they once thought would be a good fit.

You're showing up. You're doing the work. On paper, everything makes sense. But deep down, something doesn't sit right anymore. And maybe, for the first time, you're starting to ask if stability should cost you this much of yourself.

If you're still in a 9–5 and questioning whether it's right for you, this isn't a call to quit. It's a call to pause and reflect.

Ask yourself:
- Am I staying because this still serves me, or because I'm afraid to leave?
- Am I building a life that's steady, or one that's just familiar?
- Is this structure helping me grow, or quietly shrinking me?

There's no shame in staying. But there's also no safety in ignoring what you already know.

Real security is something you create, with courage and intention.

# Chapter 3

# *Steady over Moody*

## Mood Swings Can't Run a Business

If Anthonia could lie in bed with an IV drip line taped to her wrist—barely able to sit upright—and still stay awake at 1:00 a.m. to book airline tickets and resolve client issues, then surely I could send one follow-up email without needing the stars to align.

That thought hit me one morning as I sat in front of my laptop, wrapped in a blanket of excuses. All I needed to do was follow up on a quote. Five minutes of typing. Seven if I wanted to sound cheerful. But my mood was unavailable. My energy felt allergic to action. Suddenly, everything felt too much.

I opened Instagram. Closed it. Stared at the client's brief like it was written in Latin. Debated lighting a candle for inspiration. Then I remembered my late sister.

Anthonia ran a travel business with elegance and edge. Sickly, yes. But sharp. Disciplined. Efficient. Unflinchingly committed to her clients—even when her body was failing. And there I was, in perfect health, letting a mood delay momentum.

That morning, I made a mental note: My business cannot run on how I feel today. It has to run on how I perform, regardless of my mood.

This is the reality of building a business.

You can be brilliant and still inconsistent. Talented and still tangled in your emotions. You can be building something powerful and still feel like cancelling your entire business on a Wednesday because someone didn't reply to your message with enough exclamation marks.

The problem isn't your feelings. It's when your feelings become the CEO.

Your business doesn't care if Mercury is in retrograde. It needs the invoice sent. It doesn't care that you're overthinking your caption. It needs a post. It doesn't care if you're doubting your gift today. It needs direction. It needs you to build a platform strong enough to carry your creativity through the mood swings.

When you're having a good day, it should feed the system. When you're having a bad day, that same system should carry you.

Remember, you are the rhythm. You are the tone-setter. You are the consistency your business is waiting for.

Save the mood for the stage. Right now, lead the setup.

Anthonia would have.

## The Business Is Tired of Waiting on You

How can your business grow if everything still depends on your ability to focus?

The business wanted to expand, but you needed a nap. The business was ready for systems, but you were deep in a scroll hole, telling yourself it was research. In reality, you were buried in other people's content while the things that could actually move the business forward remained untouched.

Sound familiar?

You have the tools, the audience and the offers. But what you don't have is a decision.

A decision to stop tinkering and start trusting the process.

A decision to stop holding your business hostage to your personal drama.

A decision to stop waiting until you feel like a CEO before you behave like one.

You say you want to grow, but you treat your business like a weekend project. You say you want ease, but you refuse to delegate because no one else 'gets it'. You say you're tired, but you micromanage everything down to the font size. At some point, something has to give. And too often, it's your energy, your income or your team's respect.

If your business had a voice, it would probably ask you to get out of the way, because you're doing too much of the wrong things, for too long, with too little clarity. Your business needs focused leadership. It needs a builder who's willing to let it run—even when their energy isn't perfect that day.

I learned this the hard way. I didn't realise how much I was hiding behind 'waiting for inspiration'. I believed that if I just gave it time, the perfect ideas would land. But while I was waiting, the work was falling behind.

More times than I can remember, I delayed key decisions until the last minute because I didn't feel ready. I held back on approving designs and ordering materials—putting the team under pressure, costing me peace of mind and risking the final outcome.

What I didn't realise was that waiting to feel inspired was costing me more than making a decision ever did. It was draining my team, diminishing my confidence and delaying my work. Something had to change. If I wanted to lead efficiently and deliver consistently, I had to learn habits that could make this work, even when I didn't feel like working.

This is a call to get out of your own way.

The business is ready. The real question is: Are you?

**Pretty Work. Sloppy Process.**

The brief was clear. The mood board was approved ahead of time.

But somehow, on the day of the event, two props were missing, one team member was unfamiliar with the venue location, and the table layout was still being finalised at 3:00 a.m.

The final setup? Beautiful. The client? Delighted.

But behind the beauty was panic. The kind that comes from last-minute fixes, rushed decisions, and tasks that should have been done earlier but weren't, simply because I kept putting them off. I just wasn't in the headspace to deal with it. I kept waiting for a better moment. For motivation to kick in. For a day when I felt more up to it. But the work didn't wait. It piled up until it became urgent.

That's the danger of emotional timing. It delays what should be routine. It turns simple preparation into a burden. And it convinces you that brilliance will always save the day. Until it doesn't.

You can be producing beautiful work and still be building in chaos. And because the results look good, no one sees what it cost you behind the scenes. But you feel it. In your energy. In your recovery. In the way you dread every setup because, deep down, you know it shouldn't be this hard.

When your workflow is ruled by your emotional weather, the work becomes heavier. The process becomes unpredictable, and your team members become reactive.

That event wasn't unusual. I had been working like that for a while, swinging between moments of excellence and long stretches of avoidance. Hiring more talent wouldn't have fixed it. What I needed was consistency, and that doesn't come from feeling ready. It comes from showing up anyway.

If you only move when it feels right, you'll keep getting results that look good but cost too much to maintain.

Consistency is achieved when we stop letting our emotions lead and commit to showing up—regardless of how we feel.

## Leadership Fog Begins with You

The way you show up as a leader affects how things get done.

One week, you are hands-on. The next, you have disappeared. Some days, you want initiative. Other days, you are annoyed they didn't ask first.

It may not be intentional, but it creates a pattern. A rhythm no one can follow. And over time, it creates fog.

As your business grows, your mood, rhythm and focus start to shape the tone of the work, especially when others are involved.

You may think you're just passionate or detail-oriented. But what your team experiences is uncertainty. They don't know if something is approved or if you are still silently editing it in your head. They wait longer to move. They stop showing initiative. They learn that nothing is final until you touch it. And even then, it might change.

You might be the one doing the correcting. But you're also the one creating the confusion.

Sometimes, it's your unpredictability that creates the fog. You are tired, so you snap. You are overwhelmed, so you go quiet. You are behind, so you start micromanaging. To the people around you, it starts to feel like they are walking through your moods, not your leadership.

Even if you don't have a team yet, you might still be sending mixed signals. To clients. To collaborators. To yourself. Promising ease but delivering chaos.

You can be talented and still unclear. You can be gifted and still inconsistent. You can be passionate and still hard to follow.

What you need is a moment of awareness. A pause. A decision to lead better. Because fog doesn't lift on its own. You have to clear it with consistency. You won't always get it right. But you can choose to stop hiding behind being too busy or too tired to lead clearly. Your team, now or in the future, deserves that. So does your vision.

# *Builder's Note*

## Leadership Self-Assessment
Rate yourself on the following statements using this scale:
1 – Never | 2 – Rarely | 3 – Sometimes | 4 – Often | 5 – Always

Be honest. This is not a pass/fail test. It's a clarity checkpoint. Write your scores beside every statement.

## Leadership Scorecard
- I communicate clearly and consistently with my team.

- My team understands their roles and what success looks like for each one.

- I follow a predictable process for onboarding and project kickoffs.

- Tasks and responsibilities are documented, not only discussed in chat.

- I delegate based on insight, not urgency.

- My business can operate for at least two days without me micro-managing.

- Team members know where to locate essential files, timelines and briefs.

- Feedback is given proactively, not only when there's an issue.

- There's space in our system for people to grow.

- I model the kind of leadership I'd want to work under.

- Team members feel safe to speak up, give feedback or share ideas.

Score Interpretation

**46–55: Legacy Builder:** You're creating the kind of business people want to grow with. You lead with clarity, purpose and trust.

**36–45: Capable but Capped:** There are processes in place, but your leadership habits might still be limiting your growth. Improve what's effective and address what's draining you.

**26–35: Hustle-Heavy, System-Light:** You're still depending on instinct rather than systems. The vision is clear, but until you implement systems, the burden will continue to fall on you.

**11–25: Leader in Survival Mode:** You're overwhelmed. Pause. Rethink your leadership rhythm. Your business is waiting for a different version of you.

# Chapter 4

# *Faith, Fear and Free Work*

**Faith**

There's a kind of faith you need to build something that doesn't exist yet.

The kind that keeps you going after sending a quotation and hearing nothing back. That makes you refresh your inbox, just in case. That tells you to keep showing up when logic says, 'Try something else'.

Starting a business doesn't always feel like a bold leap. Sometimes, it's made up of a string of small, hesitant steps, especially when everything around you says you should be chasing something more predictable.

The early days rarely feel glamorous. They look like prepping for a project you're not sure will get approved. Spending your last bit of money on an office space, hoping the clients will come. Getting dressed and showing up to secure a major job without prior experience, but showing up like a professional anyway.

The frustration arises when faith doesn't immediately look fruitful. You reach out to clients, and there's no response. You know you're talented, but talent doesn't seem to be enough to land you a gig. It starts to feel like there's always a long, uncomfortable quiet season between projects.

But sometimes, a quiet season is space. Space for growth, for refining your systems, for building confidence. If everything had come too quickly, many of us wouldn't have lasted.

Real faith prepares. It practises, sharpens and gets ready long before the opportunity arrives. It is the behind-the-scenes labour no one notices.

I remember one day sitting in my workspace, a small corner in my living room I had carved out, with a table and some notes. I hadn't had a job in weeks. The enquiries had slowed. The last two clients had said they'd 'get back to me'. I stared at my computer, knowing full well that refreshing my email every ten minutes wouldn't change anything.

But that afternoon, I got up and reviewed my last job. I rewrote my checklist. I improved my quotation template. I repackaged some of my props and edited a few photos. No client had asked for any of that. But I knew the time would come. And when it did, I didn't want to still be scrambling.

Another thing that helped me stay focused was journaling. Writing down how I wanted my business to feel. How I wanted to show up: prepared, poised, solution-oriented. Writing it down made me act with more intention.

Faith is acting like clients are coming. It's speaking like the business is real. And preparing like the doors will open. Because your work deserves to meet opportunity fully prepared.

Faith makes us dream. Intention helps us act like the future we want is already on its way. If you stay true to the vision and consistent in your small actions, you will look back and realise you were building something far stronger than a hustle. And when the calls come in, the bookings pick up and the recognition grows, you'll be glad you took the time to prepare.

Sometimes faith is the only map you need—to take the first step and then to keep going—when fear and doubt pull at you.

## Fear

Fear is sneaky.

It doesn't always show up as panic or paralysis. Sometimes it disguises itself as logic, humility, or even responsibility. It whispers things like, 'Maybe you're not ready', or 'Let's wait until things are more stable'.

It sounds rational. It even feels protective. But if left unchecked, fear will quietly take the wheel, steering every decision you make in your business.

Fear doesn't always say, 'Don't start'. It negotiates:

Charge less; you're still new.

Take the client; you need the job.

Don't post that; it's not perfect.

Soon enough, your business revolves around keeping fear comfortable.

The problem isn't fear. The problem is when we don't notice that it's running the show.

One of the biggest areas where fear hides is visibility. It tells you to wait until your photos are better. Until your audience is bigger. Until you feel more 'ready'. But visibility is more about presence than perfection. If no one sees you, they can't trust you. And people trust consistency, not perfection.

Fear also creeps into pricing. It says, 'Who do you think you are to charge that?' So you explain too much, apologise, or overload your offer to make it feel worth the price. And once your client senses that doubt, they start negotiating, because the door was left open.

Fear doesn't mean you're failing; it means you're stretching. It shows up when you're doing something new, risky or bigger than before. The goal isn't to eliminate it; it's to learn how to move forward despite it. You can't build a successful business if decisions are made from a place of fear.

Fear prepares you for rejection but never for success. You rehearse, 'What if it doesn't work?' so often that you forget to plan for, 'What if it works?'

Fear also tempts you to overwork just to feel worthy. It says, 'If I don't do everything myself, I won't be seen as hardworking'. So you take it all on.

One thing that helps is gathering evidence: looking back at the work you've done, the clients who were satisfied and the referrals you've earned. Fear thrives when you forget how far you've come. Confidence grows when you remember.

Fear lies. It tells you confidence comes after success. But confidence is something you practice on the way to success. You show up like a pro even when there are barely bookings. You price your services boldly even when your audience is still small. You speak clearly about what you offer even if you're still refining it. That's real confidence. And that kind of confidence? Fear hates it.

Over the years, I've learned to acknowledge fear, but I don't let it dictate my actions. I ask myself, 'What decision would I make if fear wasn't involved?' Then I take one small step in that direction. I send the quote, post the photo, raise the price slightly, say no to the client who keeps moving the goalpost.

Each step weakens fear's grip, and over time, what once made hands tremble becomes second nature.

You'll remember the risks that changed your life, not the fear that almost stopped you.

So, yes, fear will show up. But you decide who's in charge.

Great businesses are built by people who keep moving forward despite fear.

## Free Work Driven by Fear

Fear doesn't only hold you back. Sometimes, it compels you to work for free.

There's a season where free work makes sense. It opens doors, builds confidence, provides content and helps you practise. Used wisely, it's a tool. But it's not a business model, and it shouldn't become your default.

Free work can give you room to experiment, test new ideas or build a portfolio. It might even lead to paying clients in the future. But without clear boundaries, it becomes draining. Your time, skill and energy are valuable even while you're still growing.

The key is clarity. Know why you're doing it, what you're hoping to gain and where it ends. Are you building credibility? Trying a new niche? Testing a concept?

Just because it's unpaid doesn't mean it should be unregulated. And if you start feeling any form of resentment, that's your signal to stop. Free work shouldn't deplete you.

Some people stay stuck in free work because they're scared. Scared to charge. Scared to lose attention. Scared of being seen as too expensive. But fear-led business decisions rarely end well.

Create your own personal policy. Decide how many unpaid jobs you'll allow per quarter. What kind of opportunities qualify. That way, when someone asks, you won't be deciding from guilt; you'll be deciding from vision.

Here's a simple line you can use:

'I've used up my quota of unpaid projects this quarter, but I'd love to work with you in the next quarter, if there's room in the budget'.

Clear, calm and respectful of your boundaries.

And let's talk about visibility for a moment. Free work doesn't always lead to exposure, and exposure doesn't always lead to sales. Be careful not to confuse attention with traction. Some clients will promise 'shoutouts' or 'tags' in exchange for your effort. That's fine if it aligns with your brand goals, but it shouldn't replace fair compensation unless the value is truly mutual.

The best clients don't need free samples. They need consistency, transparency and quality.

Your pricing should reflect your process. And even when you're starting, you can still charge something, even if it's symbolic. Symbolic pricing is better than perpetual free labour.

You can start low, but don't stay there too long. The goal isn't just to get clients, it's to build a business that can sustain your life and your vision.

Let's be honest, transitioning out of free work can feel uncomfortable, especially if your earliest clients came through friends, family or word-of-mouth referrals. You might feel guilty for suddenly setting prices or enforcing processes. You might worry that people will think you've 'changed'. But growth requires change. And the people who truly value you will understand. Those who don't were never going to sustain your vision anyway.

And don't fall into the trap of thinking free work only applies to full jobs. Sometimes, it appears in smaller ways: endless free consultations, late-night advice or hours spent tweaking a design beyond what was agreed. That kind of invisible labour can drain you just as deeply. Protect your time by setting boundaries in every area of your process.

You can still be generous. But do it intentionally. Offer one scholarship per programme. Take on one passion project per quarter. Build free content that educates without emptying your business model.

Most importantly, don't use free work to seek validation. It trains people to value you at zero. It keeps you in a cycle of over-giving, and it gradually diminishes your self-worth.

So, whether you're just starting out or transitioning into higher-level offers, keep checking in with yourself: Are you giving away your energy or investing it wisely? Are you acting out of alignment or out of obligation?

Remember, free work without a plan sabotages your brand.

## What Faith in Action Looks Like

It's easy to say you believe in your business. To speak with conviction about your dreams. To write the captions, attend the seminars, create the vision boards. But real belief, the kind that builds momentum, is proven in strategy. It's structuring your days, habits and decisions to match what you say you believe.

Faith, in business, is the daily discipline to act like what you're building is real, even before the results are evident. It's how you build when the bookings are slow. It's how you refine your process when nobody's watching. It's preparing for success before it knocks.

If you truly believe that your business is going somewhere, then your decisions must reflect that belief.

Faith in action involves structuring your workflow, rather than relying on clients to figure things out. It involves taking time after each job to reflect, document, improve or create systems, because you believe more opportunities are ahead and you want to meet them prepared.

Faith in action asks: 'If I truly believed bigger opportunities were on the way, what would I put in place now?' Then you do that, one system at a time.

Creating systems doesn't mean you have it all figured out. It means you trust your vision enough to make room for consistency. It means you're planning for the future you expect. And that kind of planning builds credibility with clients, your team and most importantly, with yourself.

Faith says, 'I'm not there yet, but I'm building like someone who will be'.

Preparation says, 'I believe in this so much, I'm getting ready for success to find me working'.

When you lead with that belief, you stop reacting to your business and start guiding it. Your workflow becomes clearer. Your confidence grows. You anticipate problems instead of constantly fixing them. You gain time, perspective and control. Your creativity expands because your mind isn't weighed down by disorganisation.

If you truly believe in your business, then show it in how you plan, delegate and document. It's okay if you don't have it all figured out yet. But start building like you believe it's going to work.

Faith in action is your willingness to build even when the outcome isn't guaranteed. Because the business is ready for you to show up with the belief you claim you have and lead like the future already belongs to you.

# *Builder's Note*

Self-Check

- What's your current boundary around free or discounted work? Is it serving you or slowly draining you?

- Think of one underpriced or unpaid job you've done recently. What did it teach you about your process, values or limits? Now write one sentence you can use the next time someone asks for free work, and practise saying it.

- What part of growing your business scares you the most? Name it honestly. Then ask yourself: If I acted with faith instead of fear, what's the first step I would take? Take that step this week, even if it's small.

- Where can faith show up in your daily actions? In how you prepare, plan and follow through?

Faith in action is what you do with the belief you have in your business. So, take one intentional step this week. Send the proposal. Launch the idea. It's not just what you believe. It's how you *act* because of what you believe.

# Chapter 5

# *Positioned to Play Small*

## The Humble Lie

It usually starts with a disclaimer.

'Oh, it's just a small business I run on the side.' Or 'I'm still figuring things out. It's nothing major yet'.

Sometimes it's said with a giggle. Sometimes with a shrug. But every time I hear it, I know exactly what's happening. Someone is trying to look humble before anyone assumes they're trying to look important.

Sometimes, we act like it's okay to be good—but only if we're a little apologetic about it. We show up, but not confidently. We fear that people might say we're arrogant, desperate, or 'doing too much'. So instead of building with intention, we make ourselves invisible.

We shrink. We stall. We second-guess the website, the pricing, the photos, the voice, the confidence, because we're afraid of what success might make us look like.

I remember carefully crafting a premium offer, but when it was time to promote it, I softened everything. I removed certain words from the caption that made me 'sound too sure'. I skipped branded visuals because they felt too polished and I didn't want people to think I was 'selling too hard'. The result? Silence. No one reached out. No one felt compelled to check out the offer. Because my energy was saying, 'It's not that big of a deal'. And they believed me.

Clients don't pay attention to what you're selling if you're signalling that you're unsure of it yourself. Your offer is only as bold as the confidence behind it.

The real twist is that a lot of this performance isn't aimed at the market. It's for the familiar crowd: the people who knew us before we started the business, or before the gift had language. The people who would say, 'Oh, you're now charging *how* much?' or 'Ah, you've started posting like an influencer'.

We're too afraid of being judged by the people who once knew us unseen. So, we keep our brilliance low so no one can accuse us of being too visible. We disclaim our excellence in advance, just in case they think we believe in ourselves too much. This fear is holding many gifted people hostage in average-looking businesses. And if we're being honest, the people who benefit from us staying small are usually the ones who feel most threatened when we start playing big.

Somewhere along the line, we've been sold a version of humility that equates invisibility with virtue. But hiding is not the same as being grounded. There's nothing noble about making yourself hard to find. And there's no award for being the best-kept secret in your industry.

People often take you as seriously as you position yourself to be taken. In business, 'small' can become a default setting and a long-term brand problem.

There's a difference between showing off and showing up. One is for applause. The other is for alignment. Strategic visibility is about being seen in the right way by the right people, for the right reasons.

So if you've found yourself constantly dumbing down your expertise, or prefacing every offer with a soft disclaimer, pause and ask: 'Who taught me that this version of humility was the safest way to show up?' Because it might be time to delete that script for good.

## Shrink for Who?

Some of us are overthinking visibility because we're still worried about an imaginary critic who never booked us in the first place.

We shrink because we're scared of how it might look to people who have no stake in our success. I've met business owners who refuse to say they're booked out. Why? Because people might think they're 'too proud'. Often, it's about someone from their university who used to laugh at their hustle. Or that one client who ghosted them—whose opinion they still use to measure their confidence years later.

Some of us are shrinking to stay likeable in circles we've outgrown. We're softening our offers to make them digestible to people who were never going to buy. And deep down, we know it. We know our messaging has been diluted. Our confidence rationed. Our content filtered through fear of being misread by people whose opinions have never paid our bills.

You don't build a brand for your friends. You build it for the people who are praying someone like you exists. So if you've been reducing your voice, editing your brilliance or playing the 'low-key' game for people who have nothing to lose if your business fails, ask yourself:

Shrink for who?

Because the people you're worried about? They're not shrinking themselves for you.

## Build Like You Know It's Going Somewhere

You must have seen brilliant entrepreneurs launch services with the enthusiasm of a world tour and the infrastructure of a pop-up kiosk. They have talent and ideas, but no plan to hold the weight of what they're offering.

Too many businesses are launched without a clear process or structure. They're attractive on social media but exhausting in real life.

I once had a conversation with a fashion designer who was clearly talented but deeply overwhelmed. She had gained a lot of visibility from a previous outfit she designed and was now receiving inquiries from event planners, influencers and even some celebrity stylists. She was worried that she wouldn't be able to deliver.

The truth was that she couldn't. Her work was good, but her business wasn't designed to handle that level of demand. It was set up for a few friends and some weekend projects. But now, the visibility was outrunning the gaps in the backend, and instead of feeling excited, she was panicking.

Ironically, most of the time, it doesn't require a huge investment to position your business for more opportunities. The tiniest tweak in how you show up—your onboarding email, your price list, your response time—can significantly impact how people perceive your capacity and help you handle volume with ease.

If you want your business to be taken seriously, you must start positioning it as something worth taking seriously.

## Structure Prevents Shrinking

Some businesses collapse because they grew too fast and the structure behind them wasn't strong enough to carry what they'd built.

Some early success can create chaos. You're finally getting noticed. Inquiries are flowing. People want what you offer. But behind the scenes? You're duct-taping things together.

One of the biggest misconceptions is that you have to become big before you structure things. That you can keep freelancing your systems until you hit a certain number. But then, small, messy and unstable becomes your brand positioning. It teaches the market to take you lightly.

I've seen business owners who won't increase their rates because they don't trust their team to show up well. Visibility isn't their problem. Talent isn't their problem. Structure is. Every time you find yourself avoiding opportunities that feel too big, it's because you know your backend can't support what your brand is promising. And that tension shows in how you present yourself.

You won't position boldly when you're not sure you can deliver consistently. You won't speak confidently when your process is patched together. You won't take up space if the backend is whispering, 'We're not ready'.

Structure tells the market: I take this seriously.

It tells your clients: You can trust me with more.

It tells you: I'm not building to survive anymore.

The freedom you're craving, the ease, the clarity, the confidence to charge more and show up fully? They don't come from working harder. All of that comes from setting things up better.

So, fix your backend, because it may be reinforcing the very smallness you are trying to outgrow. Let your systems support your gift, and make sure your structure reflects the level you're positioning yourself to play at.

## Take Up Strategic Space

Your gift has already made room for you. The question is: Have you moved in, or are you still lingering by the door?

The most dangerous thing about shrinking is that it often feels logical.

I've heard people describe their early brand phase as 'laying low', 'figuring it out', or 'still testing the waters'. And that's fine, unless you've been in the testing phase for five years and you're still whispering your offer like it's a secret.

At times, it's understandable. Stepping fully into your own voice can be confronting. It's like walking into a party where you know you've been invited, but you still feel the need to prove you deserve to be there. However, no one else is going to hang your brand's name on the wall for you. No one is coming to fix your messaging mid-launch. No one is adjusting your rates on your behalf. The seat has already been built for you. Claiming it? That's your responsibility.

People wait to feel undeniably ready before they show up boldly. But 'ready' is a decision. It's letting go of invisible loyalty to old versions of yourself. It's realising that being multi-talented is not a reason to brand yourself vaguely; it's a reason to build something worthy of range.

If you've made it this far in this book, you've likely outgrown the small version of what you do. You've seen it in how people respond to your work. You've felt it in the pull to refine how you show up. You've probably said 'no' to a few gigs this week because they didn't feel like the right fit anymore.

The next version of your business now needs room.

Taking up strategic space is about being found on purpose. It's about showing up like someone who knows the value of what they've built, even if they're still refining it. If your gift made room for you, your responsibility is to furnish that room. Frame the windows. Paint the walls. Put your name on the door. And open it wide.

This is the foundation. You've excavated mindset myths, challenged false humility and peeled off every soft-focus filter that keeps creatives small.

Now, it's time to build. Because the real power is in what you've created and what you're finally ready to own.

# *Builder's Note*

## The Brief

Pause here. Take inventory before you design further.

**Answer honestly:**

- What part of my voice have I been editing to stay likeable or low-key?
- Where am I still outsourcing permission or validation?
- If 100 new clients discovered my work tomorrow, would my brand be ready, or would it still be making up excuses?
- What's one simple way I can take up more strategic space this week?

## Business Reframe Grid

| Shrinking Thinking | Building Thinking |
| --- | --- |
| I'm just trying to see how it goes. | I'm designing this to go somewhere. |
| I don't want to look like I'm bragging. | Visibility makes service possible. |
| Let me start with something very simple. | Let me start with something I can grow into. |
| Let's see what people are willing to pay. | Let's price based on sustainability and value. |
| Who am I to charge that? | Who am I not to? |
| I don't want it to look like I'm trying too hard. | I'd rather be seen building than stuck doubting. |

Let this reframe grid become your reference point. You've laid the foundation. You've confronted the small version. Now, let's build like it matters.

# *Own Your Vision*

## See It Clearly

'I want a soft, romantic fairy-tale theme . . . but with a tropical feel. I'm imagining a garden ballroom, palm trees, lots of chandeliers. I think we should go with a salmon orange and pixie-dust gold. I feel this colour palette will be well-suited for a traditional wedding. What do you think, Dezua?'

She leaned in like she'd just revealed a masterpiece. She was waiting for my reaction. I smiled, pen in hand, because I'd heard this kind of brief before.

As a matter of fact, in this line of work, I've heard it all. Goose green. Tickle-me pink. Flesh peach. Chandeliers on beaches. Winter in summer. Ideas that make sense only to the person describing them.

Her ideas were a collage of inspiration, part Pinterest, part child-hood dream, part things she'd seen at a cousin's wedding. She had so many ideas, without a clear path to unite them. And she didn't need one. Because I could see it.

I could see the essence of what she was trying to create. I knew what to refine, what to cut and how to translate her scattered vision into something coherent and beautiful. She didn't hire me to echo her thoughts back. She hired me to take ownership of the result.

And that's exactly how you have to treat your business vision.

From clients to friends to industry trends, the outside world will always offer input. Some of it will be worth listening to; much of it will be noise. If you're not anchored in the bigger picture of what you're building, you'll find yourself bending to please others, adjusting your direction to chase trends, or reshaping your business to match someone else's idea of what it should be.

Owning your vision means you know where you're taking your company and you hold that course. It means you can take feedback without losing your centre. It means protecting your non-negotiables—the things that make your business uniquely yours—even when you're tempted to soften them for approval.

Sometimes, people's opinions matter. But if you don't hold the vision, they may take it somewhere you never intended to go.

Ask yourself: Are you running a business that constantly reacts to external influence? Or are you building from a vision you've chosen, shaped and committed to seeing through? The first one keeps you busy. The second one makes you unshakable.

The world might not understand your vision now, but if you keep leading with foresight, they'll eventually recognise it and know it's yours.

## Stand Like the Owner

I'm the same person who can stumble through small talk in a casual conversation, yet sit across from a potential client, pitch with precision and walk away with the job.

That boldness at the negotiation table did not appear overnight. It was built over years of borrowing confidence until I learned to carry it as my own.

In the early days of Dezua, there wasn't much to show, but I had a business name, business cards and a vision that felt bigger than the reality. When I walked into a room, I spoke and carried myself in line with where I was going, not where I was.

Standing like the owner requires carrying yourself like one. I learned quickly that charisma goes a long way in securing deals. If you don't look and speak like a serious business owner, how can you expect clients to trust you with their money?

Standing like the owner also requires presenting your work in a way that earns trust. I prepared for every meeting as if the opportunity was already mine to lose. My proposals were clear. My pricing was deliberate. I removed anything that signalled hesitation or made me appear unsure.

Even if your business is still growing, you can hold yourself to the standard of the business you intend to build. You can start by taking your role seriously enough that others begin to take it seriously too. This means leading conversations with confidence, knowing the details of your offer and following through on what you commit to. It means showing up on time, dressed for the standard you want associated with your work, and being ready to answer questions without wavering.

Over time, this posture changes how people perceive you. Clients become more open to your recommendations. Opportunities start to align with the way you have positioned yourself. Gradually, the confidence you once had to borrow becomes a natural part of how you lead.

The vision you have already claimed in your mind should be visible in the way you speak, prepare and deliver today. Stand in it fully, and let the rest of your business grow in alignment with it.

## Stake Your Claim in the Market

One of the most important early decisions you'll make is choosing where your business stands in the market and claiming that space without hesitation.

This means defining your identity clearly before the world starts defining it for you.

In the early days, I said yes to almost anything that looked like an opportunity. Kids' parties, bridal bouquets, pyrotechnics, mood lighting, anything that would put Dezua's name out there. That flexibility helped me learn quickly, but it also prevented me from being known for something specific. Clients had no clear picture of what my business stood for.

The turning point came when I began to define my lane and protect it. I chose the type of work I wanted Dezua to be known for and the level of client experience I was willing to deliver. That decision gave me a filter for everything, from the types of jobs I accepted to how I priced and promoted my services.

Your claim in the market is more than your niche. It is the combination of your style, your standards, your client base and the value you want to be associated with your name. The clearer that claim becomes, the easier it is for people to recognise your work, refer the right clients, and trust you with higher budgets.

Staking your claim also means letting go of opportunities that pull you away from the direction you want to grow. It may feel risky to turn down work, but every 'yes' to the wrong project is a 'no' to the one that could move your business forward.

When you own your vision and your place in the market early, you stop chasing random opportunities and start attracting the right ones. Your work begins to speak for itself, and your business develops a presence that others can't ignore.

**The Vision Keeper**

At the start of a business, it's easy to think your role is to manage.

To keep things organised, ensure tasks are completed and respond to whatever the day throws at you. But that's operating in management mode. It keeps the doors open, but it doesn't push the company forward.

Leadership is different. Leadership is holding the picture of where the business is going, even when the day-to-day operations seem messy or uncertain. It's protecting the vision from being diluted by short-term fixes or pulled off-course by other people's expectations.

In my early years, I adopted several practices that didn't align with the vision I had for the brand. Clients would request something outside our style, and I'd say yes to avoid losing the job. Team members would suggest shortcuts that made the process easier but compromised the design, and I'd allow it to save time. The more I did this, the more the business drifted from the standard I wanted to set.

The shift came when I realised that my real job wasn't just to manage the work, it was to guard the identity of the business I was building. That meant saying no more often. It meant turning down projects that didn't align with our values, even if the financial benefits looked promising. It meant holding the line on quality, even when deadlines were tight.

Being the vision keeper is an active role. You decide what the business will be known for, and then you protect that identity fiercely. You create the reference point for every decision: Does this align with where we're going? If the answer is no, it's not worth the distraction.

Leadership isn't a title you wait to be given. It's a role you take, one decision at a time. It's in the way you say no to what dilutes your brand, the way you protect the standard you've set, and the way you keep your business focused on the vision you first envisioned.

As you step into the next stage of building, remember this: anyone can be a manager, but not everyone can be a leader. Leaders keep the vision alive. They don't just react to what's in front of them; they build towards what's ahead. That's the role your business needs you to step into now.

# Builder's Note

### Guard What You're Building

A business can survive for a while without a clear leader, but it cannot grow into its full potential that way.

Somewhere between your first booking and your next big milestone, you'll face a choice: keep managing the chaos, or step up and lead with intention.

Part 1 has been about becoming the builder. It's been about defining the mindset, the choices and the identity that will carry your work forward. From here, we move into building the framework that will hold that vision steady as the business grows.

But before you turn the page, pause for a moment. Picture your business five years from now. Imagine it at its best: thriving. That vision is yours to protect. And no matter how many people work with you, no one else can guard it the way you can.

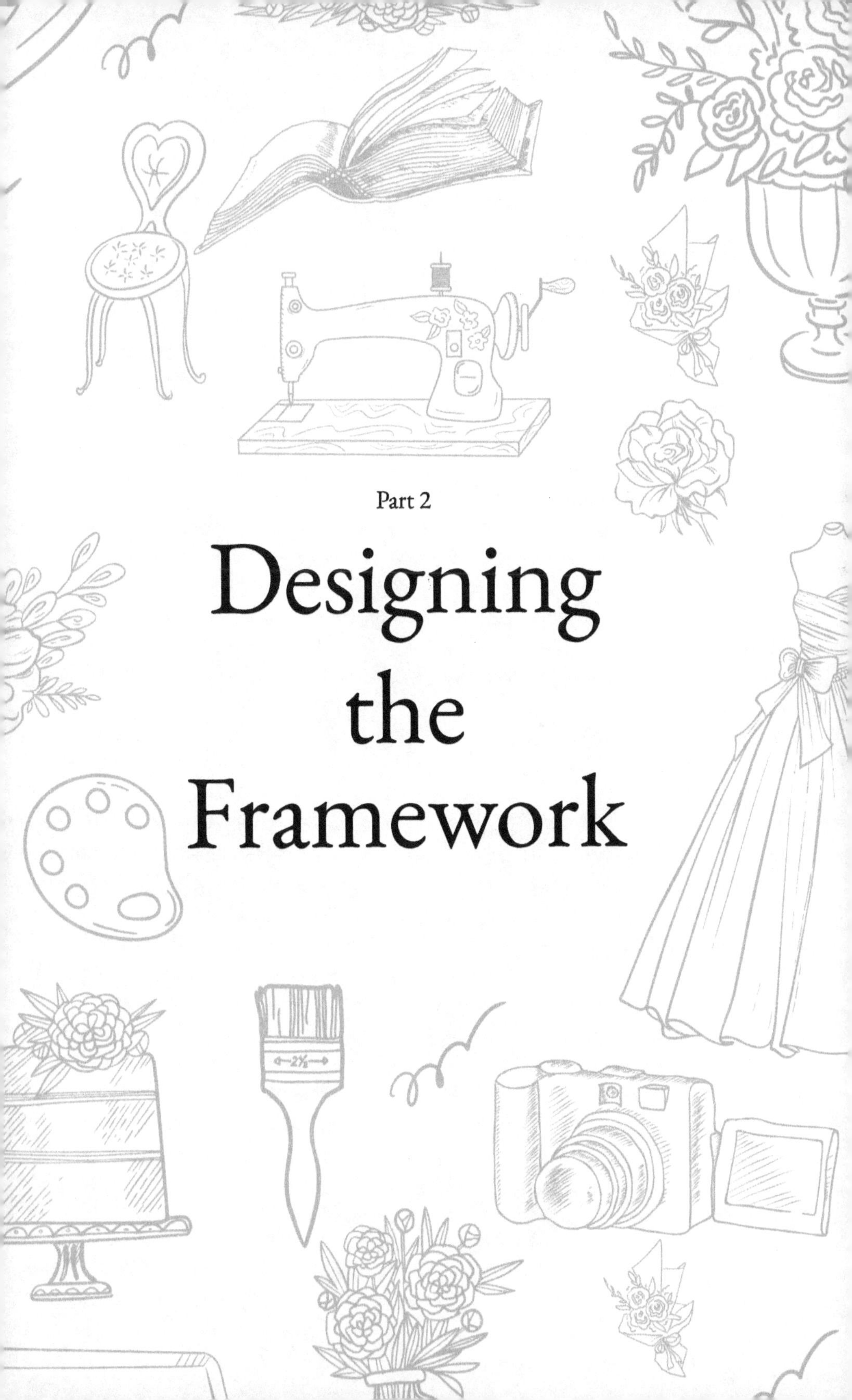

Part 2

# Designing the Framework

# Chapter 7

# *The Work Behind the 'Wow!'*

**Deliver Stability**

I was still beaming in dreamland when I was yanked awake by the loud buzz of my phone. Twenty-two missed calls. Twenty-seven messages.

Barely an hour before, I had left the venue feeling weightless, floating on the pride of what I believed was the most breathtaking event we had ever designed. It wasn't just beautiful, it was bold, refined, and unlike anything the city had seen. We'd even hired a photographer and a videographer to capture every angle, because we knew what we had created was truly magical.

Word was already spreading around town. 'Dezua just raised the bar in Benin City', someone had said to me, and I believed it.

So I dozed off in the car on my way back home, lips smiling, heart full, eyes heavy, trusting that the work would speak for itself. It did. But not the way I hoped.

One of the messages said:

'Mary, the entire stage has collapsed'.

I blinked. Read it again. Another message confirmed it:

'The couple just stepped off for their first dance and everything came down'.

I sat upright, heart thudding, every ounce of sleep gone.

Apparently, speakers had been placed directly on the stage platform—massive ones with strong vibrations. The constant pulse had weakened the structure until it crumbled inward.

My mind raced. The couple. The guests. No one was hurt, but that didn't comfort me. I had signed off on the build. I stood on that very stage hours earlier and gave the final green light. I'm an engineer, for heaven's sake. I should have anticipated it. I should have checked.

The disappointment in myself cut deeper than anyone else's criticism ever could. That day did more than humble me. It changed the way I defined 'delivery'. Because if delivery only means 'the client gasped when they walked in', then what happens when the gasps turn to panic?

We often talk about consistency, but true consistency in project delivery is built on checks and buffers. That collapse didn't happen because we lacked skill. It happened because we lacked safeguards. And when you're running a business, especially one you intend to grow, you have to build with proper systems that protect the integrity of your work.

So, I made some hard changes:

- No more fabricating without integrity checks.
- No more load-ins without platform testing.
- No more relying solely on how things 'look' onsite.

Now, every major installation goes through a final check. Every delivery is tracked with internal milestones. We audit more than the design; we audit the integrity of what holds it up.

The more successful your work becomes, the heavier the expectations it carries. And if your delivery systems can't carry that weight, you may find yourself pulling off greatness while gradually falling apart.

You need the kind of delivery that doesn't collapse under pressure. That means:

- Your team works with awareness.
- Preparation doesn't begin the night before. It starts long before that with buffers and checkpoints.

- Your brilliance is protected by procedures.

Delivery reflects the integrity of everything leading up to the final reveal. It demonstrates that the effort behind the scenes is just as solid as what appears in the spotlight.

## Can You Repeat That?

The 'disaster' of the Benin event lived rent-free in my mind for many months.

When I reviewed the project, I found the preparations leading up to the day of the event seemed smooth. Everything felt aligned: the concept, the timeline, the team. The setup looked crisp and intentional. It felt like a client's dream. It was a flawless experience. For once, I wasn't praying through setup. My team was on point. I thought I had finally arrived at something solid. Something replicable. Only it wasn't.

After the ordeal, I was determined to repeat that same design, this time sturdy and hazard-free. I needed to prove to myself that I could deliver it. I opened a new folder for this new event and stared at a blank mood board. It felt like I was starting from scratch. I thought to myself: Why does something I achieved just months ago still require so much effort to recreate? Why isn't it already documented?

The fact is that I hadn't modelled my business for repeatability. I embodied the myth that reinvention keeps a brand premium. I felt that if I didn't change everything, I would seem lazy, or worse, predictable. But the cost of constant reinvention was fatigue and operational fragility. If the magic depended on my energy, memory and mood, then I was pulling off miracles every time. And miracles aren't scalable.

Documentation protects creativity; it doesn't threaten it. Once you know what works and how you did it, you can refine it. I mean, how can you call something your signature if no one on your team can recreate it without your presence?

This wasn't the first time I had been caught by a lack of repeatability. Once, an event planner asked me to recreate one of my previous looks for her client's birthday. She referenced a photo from three years prior. I remembered the design instantly, but I couldn't remember how we built it. I didn't even remember the material source. That setup lived online, but not in my system. That should have been a wake-up call. But I got 'too busy' to fix it then, and the cycle continued.

Your best delivery shouldn't be a one-off brilliance. It should become part of your offer, something you can adapt and improve. This doesn't mean you stop evolving; it means you start building with intention. You give your work a name, you archive your genius, you create collections and you let your team rehearse excellence.

You know that look everyone loved? Give it a folder, a checklist, a rendering. Notes on materials, vendors, pricing. What worked, what broke and what needed tweaking. That's the difference between momentum and muscle memory.

Repeatability makes you bankable.

The real win isn't pulling it off once. It's knowing you can do it again, with less stress and more strategy. That's the difference between a one-time wow and a repeatable win. That's the difference between a hustle and a business.

**What They Don't Pay to See**

It was a Monday morning, years after the 'Benin Disaster'. I was sipping my coffee and trying to get my head ready for the new week, but my thoughts were once again clouded by the memories of that failed design.

Years had passed, but I still felt traumatised by that event. Every time I designed a wedding, it felt like I was holding my breath until the ceremony and reception were over. Every call during the celebration made my heart skip a beat or two.

While deep in thought, I received a message. It was Chuks, a wedding planner and returning client. He had seen the first set of photos and videos from the wedding reception we designed for him the previous weekend.

He didn't waste words.

'Thank you for the quality delivery, Dezua. Your work is always a masterpiece.'

It was the kind of feedback that should've felt like a reward and distracted me totally from the disturbing thoughts in my head that morning. And in a way, it did. But there was something else sitting underneath the gratitude. Something I couldn't ignore.

That wedding looked effortless. Every line was clean, lighting balanced, florals in harmony. But what it took to get there? Confusion.

We were now a much bigger company. The demand for our service was at an all-time high. The pressure from clients to take on jobs, especially at the dying minute, was becoming overwhelming.

What Chuks never saw was that the week before his event, I'd taken on a last-minute job I honestly should have declined. That single decision threw off the timeline for everything concerning his event setup. On top of that, two key team members were out sick and one of our delivery trucks broke down mid-transit.

Chuks didn't see the night we worked past 2:00 a.m. on floral prep. He didn't see the carpenters' error that forced us to redesign part of the entrance at 4:00 a.m. He didn't see the three nights I had gone without sleep to work with the graphics team. We were two wrong turns away from yet another disaster.

But in the end, his brief was delivered. That's what he saw. And to be fair, that's what he'd paid for. He hired me for the final result, not to share my stress.

You see, his message surfaced a truth: even after all these years, my ability to deliver still relied on personal sacrifice and constant mental juggling. My business had grown, but my systems hadn't kept the pace.

I wasn't running the business efficiently; it felt like a rescue mission every time. I had normalised operating in overdrive. I gave myself a pat on the back for pulling off magic under pressure, as if that ability was a good business model. It wasn't.

No matter how many compliments I received, it chipped away at my peace, my capacity and my growth.

It's easy to get stuck in a role where you're the answer to every dropped ball. You think it makes you reliable, but if your system depends entirely on your ability to 'make it happen', then it's neither efficient nor scalable.

Every time I pulled off another chaotic event, I reinforced a model that still required my full presence, full attention and full adrenaline to function. That wasn't true leadership. I had created a dependence system. My team couldn't step up because I was always in the middle, fixing problems. My clients didn't even realise what it cost me to produce the results they were thanking me for.

The more seamless my results appeared, the more people assumed seamless was easy. That only compounded the pressure, as my silence was now part of the promise. They had seen what I could do, so they expected that standard every single time, regardless of what was happening behind the scenes.

I treated that pressure as normal. I built my timeline around it. I even started mentoring others on how to handle it, not realising I was teaching them how to endure what I hadn't yet escaped.

Your delivery framework is what supports your work when your energy runs out. It enables your brilliance to shine without demanding anything in return. From the moment you get booked, your workflow should have a rhythm that protects you. Not in your head, but documented, shared and understood. Everything should be accounted for.

If a task appears in every project, it should have defined steps.

If a delay occurs more than once, it should have buffers.

If a team member keeps guessing, it's probably because you haven't clearly defined their role.

Nothing complex is required. In fact, your first 'system' can be a quick voice note to yourself after every job:

- What took too long?
- What did I forget?
- What stressed me unnecessarily?

That's your blueprint. Build from there.

Clients don't pay for your exhaustion, but they benefit from it when your process isn't protected. And the more you absorb, the more invisible the real cost becomes—until something eventually breaks.

That's the thing about invisible work: it grows roots under everything else. It leaks into your mood, your health and your joy. Before long, you realise you're still showing up, but with less of yourself in the room.

Let's design workflows that keep the gift flowing without draining the person behind it. Because the drain is the slow erosion of the joy beneath the beautiful work. And that kind of erosion is a business risk.

**Document the Magic**

The design process lived in my head—or so I believed.

I swore I'd remember the supplier's name. I trusted my brain to recall the exact floral vendor. Surely, I'd remember how we did that ceiling install. Then the next job rolled in, and those brilliant details were gone.

Everything lived in scattered WhatsApp threads, screenshots buried in my phone, and Instagram saves I never revisited. That's how we burn through our business margin: one forgotten detail at a time.

Because we never thought we needed systems, or we imagined we had them.

Businesses need a framework.

I know sometimes we worry about the business becoming too rigid, robotic or boring. We worry about losing *the spark*. But we need standards to protect it. When your best ideas live only in your memory, they become fragile: impossible to teach, hard to repeat and guaranteed to vanish under pressure.

Documentation safeguards creativity.

Start small. Capture what you already know:

- When should fabrication start?
- What is the correct order of installation to avoid clashes?
- Vendors' lead times?
- Approved or rejected design details?
- Who handled what in the last successful setup and how?

Translate what worked into a process instead of rebuilding from scratch.

Use what works for your flow: Google Drive folders, phone albums, voice notes after jobs, quick AARs (after-action reviews). Label project folders clearly. Name your standout looks.

Documenting it is how you build something that can be repeated and remembered and is remarkable every single time.

Make it searchable. Make it repeatable. Make it yours.

If it was magical once, it should be possible again intentionally. When that magic is captured clearly, something changes. Training becomes easier. Onboarding speeds up. Scaling feels more achievable. You no longer depend on your presence to drive every outcome. Your business progresses with or without you. Eventually, your creativity won't just define you; it will outlast you.

## Freelance Energy to Founder Energy

I was at a milestone birthday party at a well-known event centre. This time as a guest, not the decorator. But the moment I stepped into the venue, I noticed the designer. She wasn't hard to spot. She was everywhere. It felt like I was looking at an earlier version of myself.

She walked briskly from one side of the room to the other, adjusting florals, rearranging chairs, giving the lighting instructions and answering what looked like her fourth phone call in under ten minutes. She wiped sweat off her brow with the back of her hand as guests began to arrive. She was still in branded black, eyes sharp, voice steady.

Someone beside me whispered, 'She's so hands-on. She does everything herself'. It was said with admiration. And I understood why. The space looked incredible. Every table detail was coordinated. The aisle shimmered. The stage was pristine and looked sturdy; it definitely wasn't going to cave in. No 'Benin' moment here.

Her work spoke for itself. But her body was saying something else. I could see the fatigue behind her focus. It wasn't passion I saw; it was pressure. That bone-deep exhaustion that many of us know too well— from lack of sleep and shouldering every piece of the process.

It's not unusual for entrepreneurs to be so hands-on. While that level of involvement can feel admirable, especially at the start, it becomes a trap. At some point, doing everything yourself is no longer proof of excellence. It's evidence of unsustainable systems.

What I saw that day wasn't unique. It was too familiar.

I used to be extremely proud of my involvement. Sweating during setup was the price for praise. I believed that the only way to guarantee quality was to be everywhere at once. But that hands-on pride was the result of my delivery inefficiency. No one else on my team knew what to do, and no process had been put in place to support delegation.

Freelance Energy vs Founder Energy:

Freelance energy says, 'If I'm not present, things fall apart'. Founder energy says, 'My presence builds the vision, but my absence doesn't break the system'.

Shifting from one to the other changes how you show up. You start identifying the areas where over-involvement causes bottlenecks and you're compensating for a lack of structure.

That transition doesn't happen overnight. You ask:

Where am I overused?

Which tasks still need me but shouldn't?

You teach the actions and the intention behind them. You trust, gradually. You transfer ownership of outcomes, not just of tasks. It's uncomfortable at first. Your team will stumble. You'll want to jump in. But the real shift isn't about control. It's about clarity. It's about designing a business that outlives your physical stamina and makes room for you to think.

That designer I saw that day was brilliant. But I wondered how long she could keep delivering at that level if everything still depended on her hands.

The finest builders enhance their creativity by protecting it with process. When your business can operate with or without you, you've created something worth leading.

# *Builder's Note*

## Build It Like You'll Need It Again

The real work lies in the unseen steps that make a result repeatable. Protect the wow by building documented processes that deliver it again and again.

## The Signature Repeat Checklist

| What to Identify | Why It Matters |
| --- | --- |
| Three projects you're most proud of | These are your benchmarks for repeatable excellence |
| Materials used | It allows you to budget, source and plan without the scramble |
| What slowed you down | It reveals which steps need a template or system |
| What made the setup easier | It highlights repeatable wins you can standardise |
| What can be offered again as a set | It begins your journey to productised creativity |

# Chapter 8

# Great Service, Still Broke

## The Burden of Being Good

There I was again, smiling politely while accepting a payment that was four days late and a few digits short, right after the client said, 'Honestly, you're amazing. Your work is worth so much more than this'.

The compliment was generous. The balance wasn't. And somehow, I'd become the kind of professional who is praised like a luxury brand and paid like a seasonal intern.

I didn't want another round of admiration. I wanted my invoices settled without constant follow-up. I wanted my terms respected without reminders. But here I was, again, receiving a standing ovation from someone still sitting on my payment. I was standing there with a half smile, feeling shortchanged but unwilling to speak up.

When you're genuinely good, people can feel it. Your clients feel it. Your followers feel it. Other vendors feel it too. But that same reputation can limit your growth potential if you don't protect it. Because with great service comes great expectations, often undefined, unpaid and unreasonably elastic.

You'll hear things like:

'We know you'll make it work'.

'You always go the extra mile'.

'You're so easy to work with'.

'I trust you completely'.

And my personal favourite:

'Once it's Dezua, I sleep easy'.

These are beautiful words until you realise they're often used as currency in place of payment.

If you've ever delivered more than what was agreed, absorbed a client's poor planning, or carried a project on sheer willpower just to 'maintain your standard', you've experienced the burden of being good.

It's when you are hired for your skill, but end up silently contracted to:

- Be flexible with your boundaries
- Justify your pricing
- Keep smiling even when the brief changes four times
- Absorb delays, shortages and emotional acrobatics
- And somehow make it all look easy

And . . . you do it. Because you care. Because you've built a reputation for being agreeable. Because you believe in showing up well.

The uncomfortable truth? Skill alone isn't enough to safeguard your profit. Without clear terms, your talent becomes an open tap that drains more than it delivers.

Your standards should be your strength, not a loophole for unpaid work. Your clients aren't wrong to admire your dedication. You can still do your best without being taken for granted. Let excellence no longer be an excuse for overworking.

Let's start by acknowledging all the work we're doing for free.

**The Unpaid Admin Job**

It began with a voice note around 9:00 p.m.

'Hi love, I have one more idea for the backdrop. Can we maybe make it look like Santorini? Or at least give it that feel. Let me know what you think'.

I told myself it was fine; I'd reply in the morning. But then I was lying there thinking about white walls and blue domes. Already checking Pinterest.

Forty-five unpaid minutes later, I was deep into a new concept, brainstorming for the same client who had underpaid me at our last event.

This is the unpaid admin work: the part of the business that develops into a full-time role you never priced for. It's not the actual service; it's the support surrounding your service. The back-end labour clients assume 'just comes with it'. Well, guess what? Someone is paying for that labour. It just happens to be you.

Let's call it out. It looks different across creative industries, but the effect is the same.

**For event designers:** receiving new floor plans on the night before an event, reworking layouts for 80 unplanned guests, managing third-party vendors without prior notice.

**For photographers:** last-minute shoot changes, location scouting, outfit approval texts, editing timeline pressure—none of which were in the original brief.

**For graphic designers:** endless 'Can we try it this way?' emails, font debates, logo mock-ups for concepts the client isn't sure about.

**For content creators:** free brainstorms in DMs, unpaid strategy advice, edits, captions, hashtags and Reels ideas that weren't scoped or priced.

**For coaches or consultants:** ongoing WhatsApp support, extended calls, 'quick questions' that turn into full sessions.

All of it is labour, yet none of it is recognised. And because it's not defined, it's not paid.

At some point, we must decide to stop running an unpaid help desk if we want to take our business seriously. Without boundaries, we end up playing multiple roles: designer, advisor, fixer, therapist, hype woman, admin, operations manager—and that's before the real work begins.

We forget what we were actually hired to do because we're too busy making sure everything doesn't fall apart.

Every time you reply to that late message, resolve a logistics issue that isn't your responsibility, or adjust your workflow to accommodate someone else's chaos, you're paying an invisible tax: the cost of being too helpful, too available and too hesitant to say, 'That's outside the scope'.

The real risk is that unseen work breeds resentment. Resentment creates silent barriers between you and your work, you and your client, and you and your creativity.

Every hour spent on unpaid admin tasks is an hour not dedicated to what you were hired to do.

Why does this keep happening? Because we want to serve well. Because we don't want to appear difficult. Because somewhere along the line, we absorbed the idea that 'good service' means saying yes, even when it comes at our own expense. So we take it on—the WhatsApp requests, the late-night calls, the timeline tracking. We become the system for a client who didn't hire one.

So how do you start breaking that cycle?

Here's your first step:

Write down every single task you've been handling that was never quoted, never agreed on and never charged for. Make it visible. Post it in your workspace if you have to. Once you see what your clients are getting for free, you'll stop feeling guilty for drawing lines and protecting your time.

## High Praise, Low Profit

We've all seen how glowing praise doesn't always translate into healthy profit.

The thank-you message might be long and heartfelt. They might tag you in ten stories, drop a public shoutout and even promise referrals. Yet, when it's time to rebook or recommend . . . nothing.

You've been paid, yes. But not quite what the job required. You're grateful, but not satisfied—and you're probably not surprised.

This imbalance in the creative industry is concerning. People adore the outcome. They love how it makes them feel. They'll talk about you to everyone they know—until someone asks how much it costs. Then the tone changes. The energy shifts. Suddenly, you're 'expensive', it's 'a lot of money for décor'. That same person who praised your creativity starts offering 'friendly feedback' on your rates.

It's almost unbelievable how quickly admiration gets replaced by negotiation.

Compliments are cheap indeed. It costs nothing to say, 'You're amazing'. It costs nothing to repost a design. What costs something? Commitment. Paying in full. Referring you without editing the truth. Yet we often confuse compliments with currency. We believe that public admiration is a sign of progress. That going viral equals being valued.

As creatives, our work is deeply personal. We're not only selling a service; we're sharing our mind, our taste, our interpretation of beauty and story. So when someone praises that and then lowballs it, it cuts deeper. It makes us question our value. We wonder if our price is too high or our principles are too rigid.

This is what we need to remember: Validation is not revenue. We can't build sustainability on social media love. We can't grow based on potential referrals or praise that doesn't convert.

Let's audit our current situation:

Who gives you the most praise? Are they also your most profitable clients? Have you allowed flattery to hinder your pricing growth? Are you undercharging because the feedback feels rewarding?

It's a hard audit, but it's necessary.

Sometimes, clients don't respect your value because you've taught them not to. You've given them too much access, too many upgrades and too many favours. Now they love you, but they don't take your terms seriously. They don't respect your business. And it's not their fault. That's on you.

The fix? Separate the stage from the system. The stage gets the applause. The system keeps the lights on. Build two muscles: grace and firmness. You can be gracious and still enforce your fee. You can be kind and still charge full price. You can be admired and still paid.

**Kindness Can't Be the Business Model**

If kindness is what you're selling, you'll attract clients who want the feeling of a high-end experience, but not the commitment it requires.

Are you building for a hundred sweet reviews or for clients who respect your work and are willing to pay for your expertise?

By now, you've seen how excellence without boundaries drains you. This is where you change that. Build with strategy instead of constantly smoothing things over. That's how you move the work forward.

Empathy should shape your culture, not control your pricing. You're not wrong for caring. But that care needs parameters.

If your rates are always negotiable, your boundaries are soft and your policies are 'just for formality', then you've made your standards seem optional.

Here's how to change that:

1. Set Boundaries That Communicate Your Standards: Boundaries are signals. They say:

'I respect my time and my energy, and I ask you to do the same'.

'I'm protecting what allows me to show up at my best'.

'This is how I honour the craft and the team who make it possible'.

A few boundary-setting tips:

- Include a response time window in your welcome kit. (e.g., 'Office hours: 10 a.m.–6 p.m. | Replies within 24 hrs')

- Make 'Last-Minute Requests' a billable line. If it affects your process, it affects your price.

- Set and enforce a project halt clause until the balance is cleared.

- Don't begin any work without a confirmed agreement, preferably a signed one. Protect the relationship before it starts.

**2. Price Like a Professional, Not a People Pleaser:** If no one can do what you do with the same precision, speed, quality and originality, then price accordingly. Even if others could, charge for the level you're aiming for. No one can step up on a low budget.

Stop charging as if you're only covering your time. You're also covering experience, risk, infrastructure and intellectual property. Kindness can't foot that bill. Strategy can.

**3. Enforce Terms without Guilt:** Policies don't make you unkind. They make you reliable.

When you stick to your terms, clients respect the process more. You gain time for actual work. You preserve energy to show up excellently where it matters.

It's also important to note that when a client pushes back on your standards, it's not always a red flag. Sometimes, it may be because it's unfamiliar to them. You should be clear on your value and uphold it consistently until it becomes the expectation. Being clear keeps you accountable for yourself, your team and the work.

Protect the business you're building. You didn't come this far to be valued in words alone.

# *Builder's Note*

## Audit and Shift

You've seen the cost of an unmatched service. You've felt what it means to be relied on, praised, in demand, yet not fully valued.

Now, it's your turn to audit:

- Where are you still being nice instead of clear?
- Where are you celebrated but not properly paid?
- Where have you trained your clients to expect more than they invested?

Don't try to fix everything at once. Start with one shift: raise one rate, enforce one clause, rework one process, rewrite one part of your client onboarding or say 'no' where you once stayed quiet.

A few pricing reminders:

- Don't lower your rates out of fear. Increase them to safeguard the margin.
- Don't throw in extra services 'just because'. Add them to a premium package and offer that instead.

Guard the business you're building, the energy you're investing and the vision you're chasing.

# Chapter 9

# *Your Rates Are Telling a Story*

## The Discount Is Doing Damage

'Can I ask one tiny favour?' the event planner said, flashing her most charming smile.

It was two weeks before her event. The final invoice had been sent. The design was locked. The logistics were tight.

'I know we agreed on a stage design, but my client saw this other one he absolutely loves. So I was wondering if we could just . . . tweak it a bit? Maybe bring in those floating candles too?' Pause. Smile again. 'I mean, since we're already doing the work'.

I hesitated, knowing full well we were crossing into a different tier of service. But the moment was tender, and it felt easier to nod than to negotiate. So I nodded. A small tweak. Then another. Then a few complimentary rentals to 'complete the look'. The final result? We delivered a premium experience at a standard package rate.

The planner was thrilled. Her clients beamed. They gushed and posed. But then came the moment that really stung. Another guest, clearly impressed, asked her how much it all cost. Without missing a beat, she mentioned our original figure. The price before the upgrades. I watched it land in real time.

I hadn't only discounted my fee; I had discounted my value.

And I did it to myself.

Most of us don't offer discounts because we've padded our original prices. We do it because we're afraid—afraid of losing the job, of looking greedy, of being called 'expensive', of being compared to someone else who charges less and offers more.

It doesn't feel like fear though. It feels like empathy. It sounds like 'being reasonable'. It looks like 'making it work'. But what we call *flexibility*, the client often interprets as *inconsistency*.

When you adjust your price without changing your offer, you create confusion. You make your worth seem like guesswork. And over time, you begin to question it too.

Discounts, especially unplanned ones, send messages you never intended to communicate. Messages like:

- 'I padded this price, so here's the real one'.
- 'You're doing me a favour by booking me'.
- 'I'm not sure I'm worth this unless you agree'.
- 'This service isn't built on value; it's built on how you feel about me today'.

None of those may be true, but perception has a louder voice than intention.

Once a client sees your price as flexible, it's hard to make them see it as firm again. And, yes, the discount might win you the job, but at what cost? It often attracts the wrong sort of client: those more concerned about what they're paying than what they're getting. These clients push the boundaries, stretch the scope and conveniently forget the extras you included 'out of kindness'.

They say things like, 'Just this once', or 'No one else needs to know'. But someone always finds out.

I've had clients forward me invoices from other vendors, trying to negotiate. Sometimes, even mood boards and contracts. There's no secrecy or loyalty. So when someone promises not to share my discounted rate, I have no reason to trust them.

If your work can't be respected at full price, it won't be valued at half price either. You didn't build this business to become a budget-friendly version of your gift.

Now, let's be fair. Discounts aren't the enemy. Random, reactive, fear-driven discounts are. A strategic discount is proactive, planned, protected by purpose. For example:

- When you're launching a new offer and want feedback.
- When you're bundling services to increase perceived value.
- When you've remodelled your packages with pricing flexibility in mind.

That's smart pricing. That's you staying in control. But if your discount is the result of discomfort or doubt, it becomes a leakage in your business.

Quote your actual rate, present it with certainty and calm confidence. Layer in visible value and invisible effort. And if the client can't afford it, let that be okay. You are not meant to fit into everyone's budget.

A moving price tag suggests your value is up for debate, while a steady one says, 'This is what it takes to do it well'.

**Pricing Confidence**

The first time I undercharged for a major event, I convinced myself that it was a wise decision.

I told myself I was being strategic. Sensible, even. What I didn't realise was that I was signalling uncertainty, not my capability.

It was a high-capacity state funeral decoration—3,500 guests, the largest I'd ever quoted for at the time. I understood what the job entailed and the scale involved. However, I also realised I hadn't charged that much before, so I played it safe.

I reviewed the budget repeatedly, lowering the figures. When I finally sent the quote, I had reduced it to half of what the design was worth.

The client's first response was, 'Are you sure this covers everything you're doing?' He didn't sound impressed. And I had caused that. I didn't sound like someone who had the capacity to design large-scale events. I sounded like someone hoping to be booked.

The punchline? He went with someone else. Weeks later, I discovered the chosen vendor was paid more than three times my quote.

When your rate doesn't reflect the quality of work you are offering, clients become confused. And confused clients don't pay top tier.

It might interest you to know that underpricing isn't always a beginner's mistake. Sometimes, it's a seasoned professional stuck on outdated rates. Maybe they are afraid of losing referrals. Maybe they still feel they need to 'earn their way up'. Perhaps they simply haven't taken the time to review their value over the years. Being in the game for a while doesn't guarantee pricing maturity.

When clients meet your outdated rate before they meet your upgraded skills, you train them to undervalue what you offer. As a result, they'll price you at yesterday's level, not today's capacity.

Sometimes, that gap erodes trust. People don't always see a low price and think, 'Wow, what a deal'. Sometimes, they think:

- This might be a side hustle.
- The finishing may not be refined.
- They'll probably be grateful just to be chosen.

And that's not the story your rate should be telling. Your price should say:

- I've done this before.
- I've thought through every detail.
- You're in excellent hands.
- This is a professional service.

When your rate lacks confidence, you attract smaller budgets and less respect. And if your price never matures, your business won't either. Because passion can't keep paying the bills. At some point, your rate has to reflect the true value of your work. Don't price to be picked. Price to be trusted. Price to be valued. And price to deliver at your true capacity.

## Charge for the Invisible Work

Clients see deliverables, not the effort.

They don't see you spending hours before the job even begins, mentally mapping the steps to bring their vision to life. They don't see the work behind the scenes where you narrowed down hundreds of options to a seamless plan. They'll never see the emotional burden of decision-making you absorbed on their behalf, or how you made it all look effortless because you had already worked through the confusion in your mind first.

They don't see the moments when you prevented something from going wrong before it reached them. They don't see the shifting briefs you recalibrate without flinching or the internal checklist you carry like a second brain to ensure you don't drop the ball. They only see the final product.

We're taught to bill for outputs—what gets delivered, built, or seen. But the true value often lies in what never had to go wrong because you managed it. You're delivering a design, managing uncertainty, translating half-formed ideas and also providing peace of mind. You're not just charging for your time; you're charging for the relief and mental load you carry for them.

When a client agrees to work with you, the real work begins. The burden they have been carrying gradually becomes yours. Suddenly, you're the one worrying about deadlines. You're the one thinking ahead to the details they've overlooked. You're the one obsessing over alignment, tone, budget and that one tiny moment that will determine how it all comes together. And yet, many never charge for this, which is why they end up feeling resentful and undervalued.

Let's talk about something else that often goes unnoticed: your ideas. Have you ever shared a mood board or design direction with a client, only to see it appear in someone else's work, or worse, in their DIY version of your concept?

You thought you were 'sharing inspiration'. What you were actually doing was handing over intellectual property . . . for free.

Creative direction is more than just a service. It's strategy. It's experience. It's intellectual property (IP).

That sketch you offered? IP.

That project outline you proposed? IP.

That brand concept you laid out? IP.

The way you sequence your client process, from brief to delivery? That's also IP.

When you treat your work like it's only valuable once it's executed, you rob it of the weight it carries in ideation. You discount the part that makes the outcome possible in the first place.

You need to believe your service is worth every penny of your charges and even more. Because you are delivering years of experience in a single day's work.

This is the point where your rates should evolve, because you've grown and your old rates were never designed to reflect the true extent of your current service.

You're already putting in the hard work. It's time your rates reflect that.

## Can They Even Afford Free?

The call came with confidence: 'It's going to be massive. Influencers, media, major brands. We'd love to have you on board. It's not a paid gig, but the exposure is unmatched'.

He said it like he was offering me a prize or a front-row seat to opportunity. I'd heard those words before. But this time, the request felt straightforward—a small backdrop, a few arrangements, nothing elaborate. The venue was accessible, my schedule had space, and the promise of visibility dangled close enough to make the inconvenience acceptable.

I agreed.

Then the event day came. The plan had changed. The new sponsor demanded logo placement on my backdrop. Three different last-minute tweaks came through while I was still onsite, each more frantic than the last.

We rigged. We rearranged. We made it work.

By the time the event kicked off, the lighting was wrong, the setup was rushed and my design—the one I showed up to give—was hidden behind a branded banner no one had told me about.

No credit. No usable pictures. No exposure.

Just frustration and a lesson I didn't want to keep learning.

Free isn't cheap. It can cost you more than money.

People rarely value what they didn't pay for, because payment signals worth. If you're gifting your service, approach it strategically. Establish clear boundaries. Define outcomes. Protect your time. Know what you want from the project before you commit. If it's for your portfolio, ensure the outcome aligns with that goal. If it's a collaboration, treat it like a contract.

Never accept the terms: 'Do it for the exposure'. Because exposure doesn't pay your team, build your reputation or grow your capacity—unless you control the terms.

## Numbers That Back You Up

The worst part wasn't that I had undercharged. It was that I knew I had but still couldn't explain why I did it.

It was a three-day event with moving parts, detailed setups, and client expectations that grew by the hour. But I had priced it as if it was a single-day job. By day two, I was exhausted and overwhelmed because I was stretched too thin, and I had allowed it.

Sometimes, we know our worth, but our prices lack conviction. It's often a nervous guess based on what we believe the client can afford. That's why we get negotiated down. We're quoting from instinct instead of principles.

A confident entrepreneur quotes with precision. They understand the cost of delivering a standard service. They outline their offering, factor in their real hours, calculate margins and decide in advance what's non-negotiable.

That kind of creative doesn't shrink in quote conversations. They don't add value they can't afford to give. They don't enter discussions hoping to be approved. They enter ready to collaborate because the foundation is already set.

Think about how you dine at a well-run restaurant. You don't walk into the kitchen and ask the chef to guess your budget. You sit down, open a menu and choose based on clear pricing that accounts for ingredients, skill, presentation and experience. That's structure.

Your work requires the same.

Start by naming what you offer: the services you frequently provide, the signature experiences that elevate your brand and the optional extras that add a touch of sparkle.

Break it down: your team, the rentals, the packaging, the overtime, the production hours. What does it actually take to deliver your standard of work? Build your profit into the price from the start, not what's left over. Even if you're working alone, your time still has value.

Ask yourself: If I had to hire someone to do what I do, how much would it cost? View that through the lens of your own work hours. Include the consultations, the mock-ups, the prep, the corrections, the emails and the back-and-forth. Because that's part of the service too.

Design your offers to align with this definition. Organised offers. Tiered packages. Signature solutions. Customisations that remain within clear boundaries.

Profitability comes from sticking to firm principles. And it starts with truth, the truth about what it takes to deliver your best, and what it should cost to sustain it.

## You're Not Too Expensive. They're Underinformed.

How often do we hear this same line, 'We love your work, but that's way above our budget' (or its cousin: 'We'll get back to you')?

We've probably walked away thinking maybe we're charging too much. We second-guess our pricing, compare it with someone who charges less and start wondering if we should 'adjust things a little' to stay competitive.

Most clients aren't trying to insult you. They react based on what they know, and sometimes, they don't know much about your service. They've never seen a full breakdown of what your service includes. They don't understand how your preparation affects their experience. They assume the work 'just happens' because you make it look effortless.

When people don't understand the value, they default to price.

Your job is to educate without over-explaining. A 15-slide deck is not needed to justify your price. But you do need to show people what they're actually getting.

For example:

- Instead of saying, 'I'll decorate your space', say, 'We'll design a full transformation based on your theme, including 3D rendering, cu-rated props and a production team to execute to specification'.
- Instead of, 'You'll get a photo session', say, 'You'll receive a two-hour session with pre-session planning, guided posing, access to a private studio and fully edited high-resolution images'.

Language shapes expectations and defines value.

Clients aren't mind readers, so your process shouldn't be a mystery. Think about it: you've probably spent years refining your workflow. You have systems, layers, contingency plans and an internal map for delivering high-quality work. But if all they see is a final photo or a finished project, they won't understand what it took.

As a result, they compare it to someone else offering a 'similar' outcome for less, without realising that your version includes concept development, research and sourcing, scheduling, prepping, packing, vendor coordination, quality control and final execution (plus cleanup, travel and recovery). And you wonder why they're confused by your quote.

Here's how I explain it when a potential client says I'm out of their budget:

'That's totally okay. Our pricing reflects the experience and production quality we deliver. While we may not be the most affordable option, I can assure you that we're thorough. If you ever want to revisit or change the scope, I'll be happy to explore what that could look like'.

No begging. No panic. No slashing.

And you'd be surprised how many of them return, because now they understand.

Recently, I received an enquiry from a corporate client. They wanted a transformation for a conference space: a simple stage, floral touches, ambient lighting. After sending the proposal, they replied with: 'We got a much cheaper quotation from someone else. Thanks anyway'.

Two weeks later, I got a call. That 'cheaper' option had not only fallen short; they had failed to show up entirely. The clients were panicking. The event was two days away. Could I still help? Yes, I could. But this time, the price doubled because it was now an express/emergency service.

They paid it without hesitation. Because in moments of crisis, the question shifts from. 'Why is she so expensive?' to, 'Can she deliver without excuses?'

If your service is based on professionalism, experience and results, then your price is justified, whether or not the client recognises this immediately.

## The Price of Winging It

Some of us are not 'pricing' our services. We're guessing, gauging, feeling it out, relying on circumstances.

If the client sounds wealthy, we go higher. If they sound nervous, we drop down. If we're in a good mood, we might throw in extras. If we're tired, we undercharge to close out the conversation. After a while, this becomes the norm. Every quotation becomes a negotiation with ourselves.

Inconsistent pricing sends the wrong signals to your clients, your team and yourself. It erodes your business from within.

Most people don't realise how much mental bandwidth they dedicate to inconsistent pricing. You're redoing math in your head every week. You're questioning your judgement at every inquiry. You're showing up to client calls already unsure of where the boundaries are. And when your quotes lack consistency, your entire delivery wobbles.

Consistent pricing gives you mental clarity. It gives you value for your time. It also gives you emotional stability.

When your numbers are defined, you stand taller, you lead with more confidence and you perform better. Your energy is directed towards building the brand, not constantly defending it.

Let this be the last chapter where you base your rates on guesswork.

# *Builder's Note*

## Practical Pricing

Your pricing is a narrative. And whether you realise it or not, every rate you offer tells a story about your process, your posture and your priorities.

## Practical Takeaways to Build On:

1. **Standardise your base pricing**: Create a rate card with tiered packages, even if it's for internal use. Avoid pricing based on memory.

2. **Define scope before you quote**: Every quotation should be backed by deliverables, time investment and responsibility levels.

3. **Communicate value clearly**: Show what's behind the price. Present both the process and the product.

4. **Establish a 'minimum engagement threshold'**: Set a baseline below which you don't proceed, no matter how nice the client appears.

5. **Document your add-ons and boundaries**: Clearly outline extras, rush fees and revision terms so that every 'just one more thing' becomes billable.

6. **Stop offering 'free' that costs you**: Be intentional with generosity, not driven by pressure or fear.

7. **Rehearse your quote script**: Practice stating your prices with the same confidence as you say your name.

The next time a client asks, 'How much?' Don't flinch. Smile, and name your price like it's already earned.

# Chapter 10

# *One Head, Too Many Hats*

## The Illusion of Control

It was a Wednesday morning, and I was on a client call trying to sound like someone who had slept more than two hours the night before.

In reality, I was juggling mental tabs all through the night: calculating how many centrepieces hadn't returned from the last setup, tracking a fabric order that should've arrived days ago and silently hoping a client payment would reflect before Friday.

The call ended. But my day didn't. A staff member needed caption approval. A bride's sister was asking for a discount—again. Logistics was on the phone asking if they could offload items into a different space. Then came the WhatsApp message from a new client: 'Hi dear, just checking in. Have you started working on my mood board?'

It was clear the business was being steered in the wrong direction. I embodied it; every thought, every decision, every ounce of my energy was wrapped into it. And while I could handle it all, that ability was exactly the problem.

In those days, I thought my multitasking meant I was thriving. But deep down, I knew I was just trying not to sink. The hustle looked impressive from the outside. But on the inside, I was always one missing cable tie away from a meltdown. Every day ended in exhaustion. And somehow, there was always something left undone.

It starts innocently. The habit of doing it all. You say 'let me just handle it' once . . . then again . . . then always.

Before long, inquiries feel heavy because each one feels like one more load to carry. You micromanage things you shouldn't even be involved with. Your team becomes dependent on you for every single decision because you've trained them to be, and as a result, business growth stalls.

'No one can do it like I do'. That's the trap. Even if it's true, what happens if you step back? What happens if you take a break? Or fall ill? Does the work pause or collapse?

Reliability is not the same as building resilience. What you've done is build a system that can't function without you.

Your team can't grow if you don't let go.

You're the visionary. The one with ideas, direction and the blueprint. But when you're buried in details, your focus shifts from leading to firefighting. And if you're always holding the fire hose, you'll never design a fireproof system.

Some parts of the business require your unique insights, while the rest only need your permission to be delegated.

You built this business because you believed in a special kind of magic—one that only you can create. That magic doesn't come from doing everything. It comes from doing what only you can do, and protecting the space to do it well.

Delegation is a sign you're building something that's meant to outlast your energy on any given day.

Strong businesses are built by people who let go of the right things so the most important things can grow.

## Tasks vs Roles: Why Delegating Isn't Enough

I figured out how to delegate the work, but not how to do it right.

I'd send a to-do list to my team. Ask a staff member to follow up with a vendor. Let someone else supervise the setup. On paper, it looked like work was being shared. Technically, things were getting done. In reality, I was still the hub every spoke connected to.

I was the one chasing updates, adjusting tone, checking timing and monitoring every detail. I had succeeded in delegating instructions, but the weight of ownership never left my shoulders.

There's a difference between asking someone to do a task and assigning them a role.

- A task is, 'Send this invoice'.

   A role is, 'You're in charge of all client billing'.
- A task is, 'Follow up with the florist'.

   A role is, 'You're managing all vendor relationships on this project'.

Tasks get done in the moment. Roles create accountability over time.

Delegating tasks feels productive until you realise you're still deciding what happens next, how urgent it is and how good it needs to be. Also, if you're still writing captions and confirming truck times, who's holding the vision?

Roles build ownership. Tasks build dependency.

When you assign someone a role, you're giving them scope, authority and the expectation to lead an area without waiting for you to set the pace. And when people own outcomes instead of actions, three things happen:

1. They think proactively.
2. They create systems that help you.
3. They start spotting gaps you've been too busy to notice.

Most of the chaos in your workflow now comes from unclear responsibilities. Everyone's helping, but no one's taking ownership.

Delegation without structure increases your exhaustion. A clear workflow where each role is defined and documented is what transforms delegation into relief. It's what gives you the confidence to say yes to the next big project without mentally calculating how much sleep it will cost you. It's what ensures you're not the only one who can 'make things happen'.

What's on your plate that should be on someone else's desk?

Ask yourself:

- Who is responsible for client onboarding from start to finish?
- Who's tracking logistics and reporting delays without being asked?
- Who updates the inventory list or supplier pricing?

If the answer to all of that is, 'Me', you haven't delegated. You've multiplied yourself into multiple stressed versions.

Delegation fails when:

- Outcomes aren't defined
- Instructions arrive last minute
- The learning curve isn't allowed to happen
- You take over the moment there's a mistake

Instead, try these words: 'You're in charge of all the site visits this month. You'll do the first one with me, then I'll step back. You'll send me notes after each one, but this is now yours'.

That's how you delegate; that's how you build.

Let's trade errands for ownership and build a team that moves the vision forward without waiting for you to push every step.

## Create Roles, Not Rescue Plans

I've done it too. Waited too long to hire. Tried to manage too many things at once. And then, in a moment of frustration—usually after a chaotic event—I'd say, 'I need someone now. Anyone'.

That's how you end up recruiting help instead of building a team. You get temporary relief but no real progress. Before long, you're back in the same situation, with a bigger payroll.

I found that when I hire in reaction instead of with intention, this often happens:

- I spend time training someone I don't intend to keep.
- I can't explain the role clearly because I barely know what it should be.
- I end up doing all the heavy lifting while someone shadows me.
- I spend more time supervising than being productive.

Panic hiring costs more than money. It drains sanity, complicates operations and forces the entire business into emergency mode every time the pressure kicks in.

'I need help' sounds harmless until you realise you've said it six months in a row. The longer you avoid the work it requires to fix the core issues, the longer you stay stuck in emergency mode. And emergency mode takes a toll.

Here's a quick contrast between reaction hiring and intentional hiring:

Survival-based hiring: 'Help me finish this job'.

Vision-based hiring: 'Here's the role I need to grow the business'.

Survival-based hiring: No clear deliverables

Vision-based hiring: Defined KPIs and responsibilities

Survival-based hiring: Hired mid-crisis

Vision-based hiring: Hired with onboarding and ramp-up time

Survival-based hiring: Team stays reactive

Vision-based hiring: Team becomes reliable

Survival-based hiring: Short-term relief

Vision-based hiring: Alignment that lasts years

A survival-based hire puts out a fire. A vision-based hire builds a fireplace.

What, then, are you really building? You're building an ecosystem, a network of people who hold pieces of the vision. Which means you need:

- Job descriptions, even for a single employee
- Clear expectations, even for freelancers
- Boundaries and outcomes that are written down, not just remembered

Every rushed hire weakens the structure you're trying to create. Sometimes, the solution isn't getting more people; it's getting clearer processes. Build roles, not rescue teams.

**Support Isn't a Luxury, It's a Lever**

In the real world, businesses are supported by teams.

Founders have assistants. Designers have production teams. Coaches have client managers.

That's smart. It's strategic.

But too often, help is treated like a guilty pleasure. As if it's something you earn only after reaching some mythical level of success. So instead of planning for support, you romanticise the solo struggle.

You tell yourself it's faster to do it alone. You convince yourself you can't afford help. You say, 'It's just me for now', like it's a temporary fix, even though 'for now' has lasted two years.

I thought this same way until I crashed.

One week, I missed an entire client proposal deadline because I literally forgot it existed. My days were a blur of replying to DMs, designing mood boards, checking on the warehouse construction and answering vendor calls while driving between meetings.

By the time I remembered, the client had already moved on. I wasn't even angry at them. I was angry at myself for believing I could do it all and still do it well. That was when I stopped calling help a 'nice to have'.

Here's what happens when you work without support:

- The business relies on your memory rather than on systems.
- Deadlines begin to slip due to disorganisation.
- The most important things (client experience, innovation, personal rest) tend to slip through the cracks.

When people ask, 'How are you holding it all together?' you can't answer, because you're not. You're barely surviving.

Support is about making life easier. It's about creating the margin you need to think, lead and grow. And it doesn't necessarily mean hiring full-time staff.

You can start here:

- **Virtual assistants:** Even 5–10 hours a week can help clear your inbox, organise your schedule and manage follow-ups.
- **Interns:** Bring in someone eager to learn and develop an alignment that benefits you both.
- **Task-based freelancers:** Project-by-project help for writing, design or site supervision.

Start by identifying where your energy leaks. That's where help belongs first.

Support shouldn't only be provided when stress is visible. It needs to be part of the foundation from the beginning. Even a small form of support can remove ten decisions a day—the kind that clutter your mind and slow your progress. And ten decisions a day is a difference you'll feel.

Growth creates demand. Demand creates complexity. Without a support system that grows alongside you, you might hit a wall. Asking for help is what builders do when they're serious about protecting their vision.

If your business is meant to last, it must be held together by more than your energy alone.

## You're the Leader, Not the Load-Bearer

I still remember the first time I watched my team complete an entire event setup without me intervening even once.

The space buzzed with activity—ladders were moved, lighting angles were adjusted, drapes fell into perfect lines, tables were set with precision. I could hear the bass test from the DJ booth and see the florals placed exactly where they should be.

From my vantage point across the hall, I could see it all. The team no longer needed rescuing.

In that moment, my role had nothing to do with instructing on where the chandeliers should hang or whether the backdrop was perfectly centred. My work had been done weeks before, when we set the plan, defined the roles and built the systems to keep the vision steady.

What I was witnessing wasn't my absence from the process; it was my presence in the preparation.

This is what leadership at scale looks like. It's when your influence extends into rooms you're not physically in, when decisions are made confidently at every level because the standard is clear and the authority is shared. It's when the culture you've built can sustain a moment without pausing to ask, 'What should we do?'

I had changed how I saw my value to the business. My worth wasn't in how many problems I could solve in an hour. It was in the environment I could create so that problems were solved before I even arrived.

A leader who builds at this level doesn't measure their impact by how many hours they give, but by how far the vision runs on its own. They set the tone, shape the structure and ensure the right people have the space, resources and trust to carry the work forward.

When you commit to this, you stop being the load-bearer. You become the architect. You start designing the conditions for growth that will outlast your daily presence.

The true measure of leadership is in leaving a mark that sustains the vision for years to come.

# *Builder's Note*

Reflect

As your business grows, your role will also need to evolve.

The systems, people and culture you design now will determine whether the work depends on you—or can thrive because of your influence.

Use these prompts to sharpen your leadership perspective:

- Where does my presence still create bottlenecks in the work?
- Which decisions could be made confidently by someone else if they had clear authority?
- What parts of my role protect the vision, and what parts just protect the habit of being involved?
- How would the business operate if I stepped away for a month?
- What structures must be in place to ensure the vision runs smoothly without interruption?

Your answers are not a critique—they are a blueprint. They reveal where your attention is most valuable and where your influence can extend without your constant presence.

Great leadership isn't judged by what you personally accomplish. It's judged by the capacity you develop, the clarity you establish and the confidence your team carries forward in your absence.

If you commit to that work now, you'll build a business that will still stand strong years from now.

# Chapter 11

# *Your Business Doesn't Belong in the DMs*

## The DMs Are Not Your Reception Desk

If you'd asked me then, I would've sworn we had locked down this booking.

We had weeks of quick, warm messages on Instagram. She said she loved my style. We exchanged ideas, screenshots and vendor suggestions. 'It's definitely you I want', she promised.

So, I held the date. In my head, it seemed locked in. But nothing official happened. No serious commitment, no payment, no confirmation. Just endless chats with her, picking my brain for ideas on design and on other aspects of her event. I would regularly joke with her, saying she would need to pay me extra for a planning consultation, and we would laugh about it.

Then one weekend, I opened Instagram and saw the wedding—my concept—styled by someone else. Same elements, different hands. I was stunned. Thoughts kept running through my head. This couldn't be right. This wasn't the date she had given me. Had I been played?

The feeling of being used wasn't justified, because the fact remained that she never booked me. Never confirmed. Never paid. We only chatted in the DMs, and I sent her design ideas and profiles of other vendors, which she did book, by the way.

I gave away too much, too soon, and failed to secure my end.

DMs are not designed to run a business. Important details get either overshared or buried. It feels harmless, like a casual way to connect.

But over time, casual exchange becomes the culture. You waste time and effort. Gradually, everything important starts to feel optional.

A professional business communication begins with a clear welcome path. Not a maze of messages across different entry points—WhatsApp today, Instagram tomorrow. Just one, the right one, that tells your client, 'This is how to work with us'.

The point is not to stop answering your DMs. When someone reaches out, thank them and guide them to the appropriate channel of communication for your business.

For example:

'Hi! Thank you for your message. Kindly fill out our enquiry form so we can get all the necessary details and respond accordingly. Looking forward to hearing from you'.

Or:

'Hello! Thank you for contacting us. Kindly send the following information to our email address (info@dezua.com) so we can prepare your estimate'.

Then you list out the important information required to give a price estimate.

Warm, but firm.

When the first step into your business feels uncertain, the rest of the experience will seem just as unpredictable. Your brand deserves better.

## Curiosity Is Not Commitment

An enquiry is not a booking.

Asking for your prices doesn't mean someone is ready to pay them.

Many conversations begin with excitement and then fade away. People browse, click and reach out solely out of curiosity. They might not be prepared to commit. Curiosity is driven by mood. It fills your inbox with questions but rarely leads to action unless there is a clear next step.

That's why managing it well is crucial. When you treat every 'hi' as a serious enquiry, you end up wasting hours chasing shadows, replying in full, sending multiple photos, explaining your process, following up twice, only to realise they were never ready in the first place.

Your role is not to impress everyone who enquires. Your role is to 'filter for fit'.

That means creating a process that distinguishes interest from intention. One that makes it simple for potential clients to share their needs but also indicates that you're operating a focused brand.

Rather than answering every question:

- Configure an automated reply with essential information.
- Invite them to schedule a consultation call if they fulfil your minimum requirements.

This saves you time and maintains a steady pace.

The right clients won't see this as an obstacle; in fact, they'll value it. People who are ready to commit want ease, not endless messaging.

Think of it as the difference between touring a venue and signing the contract. Only one truly deserves the full attention of the venue management team.

A solid process ensures your system naturally attracts serious clients, leaving browsers to linger on the sidelines.

## The Client Isn't Booked Until They're in the System

'Hello Dezua, we've just sent in the full payment for the funeral design this weekend'.

That should have been good news. Instead, my eyes widened. The date had been booked weeks ago by someone else.

Here's how situations like this unfold. Two clients enquire about the same date. One is decisive, worried about losing it and pays immediately. The other keeps the conversation going—warm, friendly, but uncertain. Weeks pass in endless back-and-forth: revising invoices, asking questions, casually telling you to 'keep the date open' while they decide. Then, one or two weeks before the event, they're suddenly ready to commit . . . and shocked to discover the date is gone.

The assumption is always the same: because we've been talking, the date was mine. But in my line of work, a date isn't theirs until there's an initial payment. Talking doesn't secure it. In fact, many who choose another service provider never call back to let you know.

A booking isn't confirmed until:

- The client has completed your enquiry form or intake process.
- You've sent an official quotation or proposal.
- They've accepted it and paid a deposit or signed a contract.

Until those steps occur, you aren't booked yet. You're simply in discussion. And discussions don't guarantee dates.

Without a clear booking process, you invite unnecessary chaos: double bookings, last-minute rush jobs and upset clients who assumed talking meant confirmation.

A busy inbox doesn't mean a busy calendar. Replace assumptions with proper record-keeping. Make your booking process clear on your website, social media and email footer. Log every enquiry in a simple system. Send formal quotes for every project, no matter how 'friendly' or familiar the client is.

As long as someone hasn't stepped into your booking process, they're not your client yet. They're a potential client. And those two categories should never be treated the same.

When every lead follows the same steps, patterns emerge. You identify time wasters earlier. You understand your true capacity without having to guess or check multiple apps. And most importantly, you protect both your time and authority. Because once a client is in your system, they're not only talking—they're committing.

## You Teach People How to Book You

Most clients aren't difficult; they're simply taking cues from you.

When people ignore your process, it's often because they've never seen it enforced. Every time you let someone bypass your system, even to 'be nice', you establish a new standard. And that becomes the expectation for the next time.

A few months after a series of messy DM dramas, I decided to slow everything down. I was exhausted from chasing confirmations, tired of being ghosted and done with people assuming I was always available for endless chats. So I did the opposite. I delayed replies. I stopped following up. I avoided reminders. I told myself that the right clients would make the effort and go the extra mile to reach me.

Then one day, someone said to me, 'Honestly, it feels like you are not interested in this business anymore'.

She had hired a different event designer and regretted it after a poor experience. She wondered why I do good work, but my response to potential clients was lacking.

I felt guilty because I wasn't nonchalant. I simply hadn't taken the lead. I sent her a quotation and said nothing else. I offered no guidance on what to do next. I believed that if she was serious, she would send her deposit. I waited for her to take the initiative. I thought I was setting boundaries, conserving my energy and being professional, but I came across as detached.

Clients shouldn't have to guess. You need to guide them on how to book your services.

You may not realise it, but you're always sending a message. Your tone, pace and language indicate how people should interact with your business. When you respond casually, they'll treat the interaction casually. When you set expectations and stick to them, they adapt.

Leadership in client relationships is more about providing steady direction.

Here's how to uphold boundaries without pushing clients away:

- If someone bypasses your enquiry form and sends a lengthy message on WhatsApp, don't jump in completely or ignore them entirely. Gently direct them back to the right process.

- If they request a 'quick estimate' without a brief, explain your policy: you only provide a quotation after the full details are received.

- If you've explained your booking steps once, there's no need to repeat them three more times. Your role is to guide, not chase.

The longer you run your business, the more you'll realise that you are the tone-setter. You have the right to design a smooth process and expect others to follow it. That's how to build something that can grow. If every client requires a personal exception, your process isn't sustainable.

Anchor your communication around two things: warmth and clarity. Clients should feel welcome, but never unsure about what to do next.

Try this:

'Hello [Name], thank you very much for reaching out! To proceed, please complete this form so we can understand your event properly. We'll be in touch as soon as we receive it'.

Simple, friendly and straightforward. No room for guessing.

When people see that you respect your own process, they're more likely to respect it as well. And when you guide the client, you secure the client. If you leave them to figure it out, someone else might step in and provide the guidance instead.

Always remember this: you're not just offering a service, but designing experiences. And that begins with how people book you.

## Becoming Intentional

A client once told me I was making it 'too hard' for him to work with me.

All I had done was direct him to the proper steps. No shortcuts. No long WhatsApp breakdowns. No emotional explanations. He was just used to the instant access and shortcuts I had previously allowed him. Before, I might have apologised or bent a little. But this time, I didn't.

I finally understood that boundaries only feel like resistance to people who benefited from a lack of them.

Many creatives confuse being reliable with being available all the time. Responding to DMs at midnight doesn't prove you care. Explaining your work hours or apologising for expecting people to use the proper channels is totally unnecessary.

Once you identify the system that works for you and your brand, stick to it.

For me, that meant rebuilding how I engaged with enquiries. I created a standard reply template for casual messages. I honoured my office hours. I committed to using one or two channels for all official communication, regardless of how tempted I was to reply in multiple apps.

At first, it felt slower. But within weeks, I noticed a shift:

Clients stopped sending me last-minute messages on multiple platforms. Follow-up calls were reduced because they knew when to expect responses. The team could see every enquiry in one place. No confusion, no duplication.

Intentionality requires discipline, but it frees your time and mental space. You stop running in circles trying to accommodate every request in every way. Instead, you lead with a clear process that sets the tone for the entire relationship.

You're not 'hard to reach'; you're focusing on where your energy generates the most value. And the right clients will respect that. In fact, they'll feel relieved knowing exactly how to work with you.

This is where your brand's processes transition from being reactive to being consistent. Consistency builds trust. And trust is the foundation for premium processes.

## A Premium Brand Has Premium Processes

Luxury experiences shouldn't be delivered with a scattered system.

No matter how beautiful your designs are or how warm your client service is, the overall experience will always feel average if the process behind it is inconsistent or unclear.

Premium is how a service feels from the very first contact to the final detail.

A high-end brand delivers three things: results, peace of mind and confidence. Clients trust that every detail has been thought through. And that trust begins long before the first quotation is sent. It starts with how they are welcomed into your business, guided through each stage and supported until the work is done.

If your backend feels improvised, your frontend will always show signs of that uncertainty.

This is what the ideal client looked like when I started refining my processes:

Michael met me at a previous event and asked for my contact details. From the very first message, I could tell he wasn't here to waste time. He filled out the form, replied to the quotation within the hour and paid before the invoice reminder went out. No long conversations. No midnight follow-ups. Just calm, straightforward communication.

I almost didn't trust it, I'd become so used to chasing clients, clarifying things twice and apologising for setting boundaries. But this time, everything went smoothly.

After the event, he messaged me. 'Thank you, Madam Mary. This was one of the smoothest event bookings my company has ever made. The finishing was perfect, and your team was very professional'.

I almost cried. A stress-free delivery?!

He valued the experience because the booking process was so seamless; he never had to micromanage a single step.

Think about the businesses you personally enjoy dealing with. The ones that feel polished, reliable and effortless. What sets them apart is the experience of interacting with them, the ease, the rhythm, the way things 'just work'. Now imagine bringing that same standard to your own brand.

Start with the basics:

- A reliable booking system that works flawlessly every time
- Templates that make your communication appear polished and consistent
- Practical timelines that safeguard both delivery and your energy
- Training your team so every client interaction reflects your standards
- Automation for tasks that don't need your personal touch so you can concentrate on what does

When you operate this way, you stop blending in with other service providers. You become the business people want to recommend because of what you do and how you handle it.

Clients who value quality will notice. And they'll pay for the relief of knowing they're in capable hands.

# *Builder's Note*

## Command the First Step

A premium client is not looking for creativity alone.

They seek certainty in your responses, in how you receive information and in how their service is managed. That certainty is created through clear processes and efficient delivery.

As you conclude this chapter, consider these questions:

- How many hours am I losing each week responding to casual DMs that never convert?
- What boundaries am I afraid to establish because I don't want to seem 'unfriendly'?
- Where am I leaking authority by booking informally?
- Do my clients know how to book me, or only how to chat with me?
- How can adopting structured systems protect my time and my brand?

Pick one step this week to move your business out of casual chats. Create a clear enquiry form. Set an autoresponder. Update your bio with your official booking process.

Do this because your business deserves a process that makes working with you effortless.

# Chapter 12

# The Cost of Being a Clone

## Create, Don't Copy

Cloning is everywhere.

Open Instagram, open Pinterest, it's copy-paste everywhere. Mood boards cloned, fonts recycled, backdrops replicated. It's the same outfits, same dramatic chair pose, same storylines. It seems like the creative world is moving in circles, with everyone pulling from the same pool of ideas.

Copying begins in the mindset. You see something working for someone else, and you wonder: Maybe this is what people truly want. Maybe I should try their formula. Maybe my voice isn't clear or cool or marketable enough. So, you reach for what looks successful, what feels safe, what already exists. Gradually, you stop creating for your vision and start creating for validation.

Every time you clone someone else's idea, you silence your own. This is the real cost: losing your authentic voice.

Sometimes, it's subconscious. You liked something. You saved it. Without realising it, you began to rebuild it, piece by piece, under your name. You called it 'inspired by', but if you really zoom in, it's the exact idea, tone or aesthetic, customised with your colour palette.

However, you don't build brand power by borrowing someone else's backbone. It may get the likes and compliments. But it won't take you far. When the trend changes, the algorithm shifts and the original creator evolves, what will you do next?

The problem isn't a lack of ideas—it's a lack of ownership.

It takes courage to say:

'This is how I see it'.

'This is how I design it'.

'This is what I believe belongs in the experience I'm creating'. Originality can be as simple as adding your own perspective to concepts that already exist. It's the way you combine familiar elements, interpret ideas differently or present them with your personal touch that makes your work stand out. What sets you apart is not whether the concept has been seen before, but the way your voice, taste and vision transform it into something that carries your imprint.

That's the difference between following trends and setting a standard.

The creative industry is starving for fresh interpretations. So let's create more and copy less because the world needs our bravely filtered, strategically executed and fully owned point of view.

**Inspiration Overload**

This is how it always begins: you sit down to create. Blank screen. Blank canvas. Blank slate. But before long, your fingers start scrolling. One image leads to another. A reel turns into a thread. A mood board grows into ten open tabs. And just like that, your ideas are surrounded before they have a chance to speak.

This is the danger of over-inspiration: you don't even notice when it becomes noise.

In today's artistic world, you're always absorbing. Stylists track trends. Writers keep tabs open with competitors' headlines. Digital artists save colour palettes. Event designers pin centrepieces from Dubai, Mexico and Italy. Everyone is sourcing. And while it feels productive, it's often the very thing that dulls our voice.

We think we're fuelling our creativity, but we're actually outsourcing our confidence.

There's a loop we creatives fall into. It feels like an inspiration trap. We browse for ideas, save a dozen examples, feel a spark, but hesitate to move forward without checking what others have done. Before long, we end up more stuck than when we began. This slows us down and teaches us to mistrust our instincts. We start believing our ideas are only valid if they're validated by current trends.

If you look closely, you'll spot the signs. It's when you can't begin a project without seeing what's already out there. It's when your creative direction changes based on what's currently trending. When you feel a low-level anxiety the moment your ideas feel 'too different'. When your final product mirrors your references more than your original intent. And when you finish projects that look great but feel flat.

Copying someone else's work isn't fulfilling. And when something feels too familiar, it can lose the magic it was meant to have, no matter how polished the delivery is.

It's like hearing a comedian tell a joke you've heard before. You might still laugh politely, but there's no spark, no surprise. The delivery might be polished, but the punchline doesn't land the same because you already know where it's going. That's what happens to your work when it leans too heavily on other people's ideas: it looks fine, but it doesn't make anyone feel something new.

Originality attracts attention because it stands out in a sea of sameness. It also fosters alignment—it draws the kind of clients who value your perspective, trust your unique view and seek more than a mere polished imitation.

Originality must be guarded. If you want to prevent being overwhelmed by artistry, you need tools that help you design from within—tools that not only prevent your ideas from being drowned out but also give them space to develop. Without these tools, even the most brilliant concept can be diluted, forgotten or replaced by what's trending.

Here's a simple five-part framework to help us create before we consume:

1. **Build before you browse:** Sketch, map or record a voice note of your raw concept before you search.

2. **Timebox your inspiration:** Set a timer. Twenty minutes max. After that, you're no longer researching. Remember, the deeper you scroll, the easier it is to forget your own direction.

3. **Archive your instinct:** Start a personal archive, your own collection of sketches, captions, scribbled ideas or voice memos that feel true. These are your artful fingerprints. They're unfiltered and original.

4. **Study your signature:** Every creative has patterns. Identify yours. Perhaps you prefer bold contrasts or subtle elegance. Maybe you consistently use warm tones, dry humour or minimal lines. Record them. Recognising your patterns transforms style into strategy.

5. **Create from questions:** What do I want this to say? Who is this for? What story am I telling? Let curiosity drive the project. When you build from questions, you find your work has depth.

There's nothing wrong with studying what's out there. But there's a difference between learning from others and losing yourself in them. At some point, you'll have to decide: will you keep replicating what's safe, or will you start trusting what's yours?

The work that stands out in your industry won't come from your saved folder. It will come the moment you turn down the volume of everything you have seen and fully embrace the sound of your own ideas, trusting that it is enough.

## When Clients Commission a Clone

'Can you do this?' she asked as she flipped her phone around.

It was a photo of a beautiful design. It was polished, dramatic, stunning. A designer's masterpiece. A shot lifted straight from Pinterest.

I responded, 'Yes, I can. But it's not my style. I can use it as inspiration and create something different but equally beautiful'. She nodded, we agreed and we moved on.

The next morning, my phone lit up with a string of messages. She couldn't stop thinking about the original design. She wanted it exactly as it was, with no changes and no reinterpretation. I tried every angle to win her trust, to show her I could create something just as stunning in my own way. Nothing worked. And just like that, I was no longer being hired to create; I was being hired to replicate.

Sometimes when cloning is client-driven, it's not always framed as copying. It's often disguised as, 'I really love this look'. But if you unpack it, what you'll find is a client asking you to build on someone else's blueprint.

It happens more often than we'd like to admit. And it's rarely malicious. The client thinks they're helping by offering ideas. They want something 'beautiful', 'trendy', 'just like that other one'. But what they're really doing—without realising it—is asking us to borrow someone else's brilliance and pretend it's ours. And if we're not careful, we'll always say yes.

Why is it so easy to say yes?

If we're honest, turning down a paying client is tough. You want the booking. You want the testimonial. You want to appear flexible and accommodating. And most importantly, you want to avoid being labelled 'difficult'.

So you talk yourself into it:

'It's just one project'.

'The client will be happy'.

'I can tweak it slightly'.

'No one will really know'.

But *you'll* know. And that compromise doesn't stay quiet. It becomes a pattern. One where your portfolio starts to look like a patchwork of other people's ideas. One where you're praised for execution but not respected for imagination. One where you're working constantly but not building anything recognisably yours.

So, how do we break out of this pattern?

Most clients don't mean harm. They simply haven't been taught the difference between inspiration and identity. So we need to educate them.

Here's how:

1. **Honour their intent:** Instead of dismissing the reference, ask what they like about it. The colour story? The mood? The simplicity? The opulence? Extract the reason behind the image and use that to guide your concept.

2. **Reframe your process as a signature experience:** Say things like, 'I love that you want something elegant, but instead of copying this exact look, I'd love to reinterpret it in a way that reflects your event and my creative direction'. That way, you position yourself as a collaborator, not a replicator.

3. **Show the risk of replication:** Explain kindly, 'If we copy this design, we risk looking like a version of someone else. And that might cheapen the uniqueness of your event'. Make originality feel valuable, not optional.

4. **Lead with examples of your own:** Instead of Pinterest, build your own portfolio deck or swipe folder. When you show work that carries your signature, clients become more likely to trust your direction than demand a duplicate.

Copying doesn't protect you; it shrinks you.

When you constantly say yes to replication, you gradually become less recognisable, replaceable even, because nothing about your work stands out as yours. The referrals you get will be for more copycat jobs. The clients who find you won't care about your style; they'll assume you're good at making other people's ideas look polished. You'll feel drained, underappreciated and misaligned. Because deep down, you'll know you're working hard but not working true.

And the irony? The more you copy, the harder it is for your business to grow. Not only because of ethics, but because you've built a brand that no longer knows what it stands for.

Originality is the best marketing you'll ever do.

When your work carries your fingerprint, clients refer you with confidence. They say things like: 'She's the one who designed this', not, 'She can do something similar'. That difference is everything.

So next time a client slides their phone across the table, don't panic. Ask questions, extract the essence. Then do what you were hired to do in the first place: create.

When you create instead of copy, you deliver a story. And in this industry, the ones who build stories are the ones we remember.

**Styled, But Soulless**

This one time, the room looked like everything had fallen perfectly into place.

The colours melted into each other effortlessly, the textures whispered luxury, the flow carried you from one corner to the next without interruption. The light reflected beautifully off the surfaces, and the symmetry was precise. Nothing was out of order.

It was the kind of room people would photograph, post and praise. Yet as I stood in it, all I could hear was silence. It didn't breathe. It didn't hum. It didn't feel alive to me.

I knew why. I hadn't built it from imagination; I had built it from expectation. From the client's requests. From the market trends. From my tight deadlines which left little room for reflection. I leaned on formulas I knew would work. At the time, it felt practical and efficient. But I was honestly repeating more than I was creating.

It rarely begins as one big moment. It slips in through small, almost unnoticeable steps. You source for designs instead of imagining. You borrow instead of exploring. You reach for what's proven instead of taking a risk with what feels new. And little by little, the spark dims. The project looks perfect to everyone else, but to you, it feels strangely detached.

That's the cost of working like a clone. Your business may not collapse, your calendar may not empty, but you will start losing your voice. And when your voice fades, even the applause feels hollow.

I had to put in a lot of effort to rediscover my path. To cut through the noise of what was popular, stop seeking approval and grant myself permission to rebuild from curiosity. Slowly, I found my way back to designs that carried my fingerprints—work I could recognise as mine even in a crowded room.

If you've ever looked at your own creation and felt that same stillness, don't brush it aside. It's a signal. A reminder to pause, peel away the layers of what the world expects and return to the imaginations that began your journey.

## The Long Game Is Original

Originality is more than a creative choice; it is an investment in yourself.

It shapes how you are seen, the opportunities that find you and the value your work commands over time.

Creatives who commit to their own voice build something that lasts: a body of work that evolves with them, holds its place in the market and becomes a trusted reference for clients and peers.

Playing the long game means thinking beyond this season's bookings. It means building a signature so strong that clients come to you for your perspective, not for a menu of trends. It means having the freedom to innovate without losing momentum, because your work is anchored in principles that are not dictated by a single platform or passing style.

The rewards compound. Aligned clients bring referrals that fit. Your portfolio develops a recognisable through-line. Your rates rise naturally because your work is not interchangeable. Over time, you become the go-to person for projects that match your strengths, and you spend less energy justifying your value.

A decade from now, the projects you will be most proud of won't be the ones that perfectly matched the moment. They will be the ones that shaped the moment, changed others' perspectives and could be placed in any era yet still feel relevant.

That is the kind of work that builds reputation, influence and lasting demand.

Guard your originality as you would any valuable asset. Incorporate it into your process, protect it during negotiations and continuously refine it in every project.

This is the effort that keeps you relevant long after trends have shifted.

# *Builder's Note*

**Stay Original**

Start each project by checking in with yourself before consulting your references.

Take a moment to ensure the direction aligns with your vision and isn't solely influenced by external pressures.

Originality stems from the small decisions you make regularly—the colour choices you prefer, the details you obsess over and how you approach solving a problem when circumstances change. These are the elements that make your work distinctive and memorable. Safeguard them by developing habits that keep your perspective clear.

**Practical steps for maintaining originality:**

- Set aside time each month to create something without a brief or client request.
- Review your last five projects and highlight what feels most like your signature style.
- Spend less time browsing inspiration platforms before developing your own ideas.
- Keep a personal archive of ideas, sketches and concepts that are entirely your own.
- Build a short list of questions you ask yourself before approving any design direction.

When you work this way, you create a body of work that not only meets the moment but holds its value over time. Originality becomes less of an occasional spark and more of a standard you maintain.

# Chapter 13

# *Intermediaries, Markups and Commissions*

**Your Actual Price vs What the Client Sees**

I'll never forget the day a bride rang me up, her voice sharp with frustration.

'Why is my wedding décor bill so high?' she demanded. 'My friend's wedding had almost the same brief, and you charged her half this amount!'

I felt my stomach tighten. She named a figure that nearly made me drop my phone. That wasn't my price. It wasn't even close.

A week earlier, I had sent a quote, not directly to her, but to her wedding planner. The planner had pleaded for a discount, swearing the couple was on a tight budget. They were supposedly well-known, and their wedding would 'bring me more bookings'.

For the record, I've heard that line a thousand times, and I don't fall for it. I offered my standard vendor-to-vendor discount, and that should have been the end of it. But somewhere between my sharing the invoice and what got to the bride's hands, the price had mysteriously multiplied.

When the planner presented the 'final' quote, it was almost double my original figure. I hadn't even been looped into the conversation. No heads-up. No chance to clarify.

So there I was, on the phone with an angry bride who believed I was trying to cash in on her high-profile wedding. The irony? I'd been told it was a low-budget event from the start.

I have a personal rule: I avoid speaking badly about other vendors or event partners to clients. So, I let her vent. Then I said calmly, 'Venue design pricing isn't fixed. It's not a one-size-fits-all service. For high-profile events, expectations are different, and so are the designs and the costs'.

Her tone softened. 'Okay . . . so what exactly am I getting for this price?'

I listed out every premium service that could fit into the figure she had been given. She listened carefully.

In the end, I revised my invoice to reflect those premium offerings and forwarded it to her wedding planner along with a polite explanation.

Let's just say, I saved the day.

This wasn't my first experience with this. And while not all event planners pull stunts like this, it happens often enough to warrant attention.

In the events industry, referrals often come through third parties such as planners, venue managers, family, friends or other vendors. Sometimes they are simply trying to show support for your brand. Other times, they're angling for a commission.

The commission itself isn't always the villain. It becomes a problem when it's secretly added on top of your quotation and the client ends up confused about your delivery versus the price they were billed.

The clients think you're too expensive, and most of the time, they walk away. Why? Because they received a number you didn't authorise, a figure that doesn't match the value of your offer.

When you're not in control of the price the client sees, you're not in control of the story being told about your brand.

It's a silent leak. You don't hear it drip, but it results in fewer callbacks and cool responses from clients who once seemed eager.

So remember, if you're not the one presenting your price, you can't control how it's delivered or how it's perceived. And in business, perception is everything.

## Misrepresentation

Service businesses would be so much easier if everyone heard the same thing the same way. But they don't.

One person hears 'elegant décor'. Another assumes it means 'full event solution, rentals included'. And suddenly, you're starring in a drama you didn't audition for.

That's exactly how I ended up in an awkward conversation one morning. We'd secured a job through the client's executive assistant. It seemed straightforward. But when the client finally arrived at the venue, he looked confused. His tone was polite but puzzled, laced with that familiar hint of disappointment.

'Why am I not getting what I paid for?' he asked me.

Except, he hadn't actually paid for what he believed he had. His executive assistant had booked us at our minimum rate, and in an effort to keep costs tidy, bundled decor and rentals into a single figure. Two separate services had been combined into a single price without recognising that these were two entirely different scopes of work.

So there I was, attempting to explain to yet another client that event decoration and event furniture rentals are separate services; each with its own pricing, logistics and deliverables. It was frustrating and time-consuming.

To be fair, intermediaries aren't always trying to create chaos. Often, they aim to help. They want to simplify processes, maintain clear communication and present a united front. And many times, it does work. They open doors, smooth negotiations and provide access to opportunities you might not reach on your own.

But there's a catch: when your services are presented without context and reduced to bare figures on a page, things get lost in translation.

And when confusion hits, it's not the intermediary who takes the heat; it's you. That's why it's crucial to guard how your work is described and delivered.

The solution isn't to avoid collaboration. Far from it. It's to be intentional:

- Send branded proposals that clearly state your deliverables, so if they're forwarded, they accurately represent your services.
- Write clear breakdowns that explain what each quoted figure covers.
- Indicate in your quotation which services are not included to manage expectations from the beginning.

This clarifies things to anyone receiving your quote, protects everyone's interests and safeguards your brand from being misrepresented.

Because in the end, your brand's integrity is worth protecting and defending as fiercely as your creativity.

## Silent Cuts, Quiet Losses

I've seen the best and worst of intermediaries over the years.

Some are absolute gems who help you win jobs you'd never have secured alone. Others leave you nursing wounds.

One event sticks out vividly in my memory. Everything had gone beautifully. My team had packed up, the last prop was strapped onto the truck and we were finally exhaling and ready to head home. Then my phone buzzed.

A polite message, a quick thank you and then casually, he said, 'By the way, there will be a deduction on the balance because the client feels your service was overpriced'.

Excuse me?!

No prior discussion. No warning. Just a slice off my payment after the job was delivered.

I remember staring at the message, my body frozen. Frustration and disbelief swirled inside me. I felt robbed.

Later, I discovered the project manager had added his own commission on top of my original bill. When the client pushed back and refused to pay the inflated figures, guess where the deduction landed? Not on his commission, oh no, but on my fee. He walked away with his full cut while I was left holding the short end of the stick.

It felt grossly unfair. I'd done the work. I'd carried the stress. Why should I be the one getting shortchanged?

That's how it often happens. Silent cuts, hidden adjustments that no one discusses. A referral fee sneaked in, a deduction for 'logistics support' you never agreed to or costs you're forced to bear because someone refuses to pay for the venue's power supply or pretends they never saw the service charge clearly printed on your invoice.

They're usually framed as small things. A slice here, a deduction there. You're expected to understand, to be the bigger person. Sometimes, you do let it slide. You weigh the legal costs. You think of the relationship. You sigh and move on because fighting every battle could drain you more than the loss itself.

But there's a price.

Over time, those silent cuts start to carve into your spirit as much as your profits. You begin to wonder where the money is going. You hesitate on those extra creative touches you once threw in joyfully. Your work remains solid, but something starts to dull inside you.

I've learned painfully that big losses aren't always noticed immediately. Sometimes, it's the steady drip, drip, drip of small amounts disappearing.

So now, I don't make any assumptions anymore. Before a quotation goes out, I ask the tough questions. Before the job begins, I clarify expectations—even with people I've worked with for years. Because I know how costly assumptions can be.

And when I know someone expects compensation, I prefer to discuss it upfront, so we can agree on a fair arrangement and how they might benefit from the project through referral bonuses, commissions or collaboration credits. As long as it remains within a reasonable range and doesn't inflate costs for the client.

I believe people who bring me business deserve gratitude. However, that gratitude should never diminish my value or harm my brand's reputation. So, I've developed systems that honour them. I offer discounts to trusted planners and flexible tiered packages they can confidently present to clients.

These aren't rigid policies, but relationship-building tools—ways to keep everyone winning without hidden costs or misunderstandings.

As for that project manager? Let's just say, I've remained politely unavailable to his requests ever since.

## Protect the Price, Protect the Brand

Imagine your brand as a piece of artwork.

Every colour, every brushstroke, every detail tells a story. Your price is one of those strokes—a bold line that shows how you value your time, your creativity and your expertise. Yet, it's the part of the painting that people often try to touch up themselves.

Most of the time, they mean well. They may want to help you close the deal. But in their rush to 'help', they sometimes trim your numbers, soften your lines or rewrite the captions on your art without asking.

It's not always about greed. Sometimes, a venue manager may want to add your service to a package, a friend may think they're negotiating on your behalf or a planner may want to win over a hesitant client. But I've learned that price is language. It tells clients where your work sits in the market. It hints at the quality of your materials, the manpower you'll deploy and the finesse they can expect in the final result. Change the price without context, and suddenly the story is incomplete, or worse, misleading.

I remember one particular enquiry where the client approached me already clutching a number. He was certain that's what my service cost. But the figure was a fraction of what it should have been, stripped of the layers that make my work shine.

I asked him softly, 'Where did you hear that price?'

He paused, surprised. 'Oh . . . your name came up in a conversation. Someone said you'd do it for that'.

No harm was intended, but the damage was done.

This is why you must fiercely protect your brand's narrative. Clearly communicate the artistry involved. Spell out the layers of value that your pricing reflects. Minimise the chances of someone else rewriting your story. And don't avoid discussing commissions. Instead, include it in the story from the outset to prevent it from becoming an unpleasant surprise later.

This way, when someone mentions your name in a meeting, on a phone call or over dinner, the version of your story being told aligns with the one you intended to write.

## Smart Workarounds That Still Keep You in the Room

Let me reveal a secret: the real magic often happens when you're not present in the room.

It's the quick mention of your name in a meeting, the recommendation passed along in a WhatsApp group, the conversation that occurs over coffee between a planner and a client or the referrals from friends and family. That's how doors open, but it's also how misunderstandings can creep in.

Every time your name travels without you, your brand relies on someone else's words, memory and understanding. And if they don't have the right tools, even well-meaning people can derail the story you've worked so hard to build.

I've experienced being on the other side of the table several times, so I know how easy it is to misrepresent things.

There was a time a long-standing client asked me to source a massive tent for a corporate event I was designing. So, I reached out to the only rental company in the region that had the size of tent we needed.

They responded in their usual manner; only numbers pinged over WhatsApp. No official letterhead, no detailed specifications, no professional invoice. But my client was part of a corporate team that required official documentation. She needed clear descriptions and a proper invoice to present to her superiors. The tent vendor, however, wasn't accustomed to preparing any kind of documentation. They'd never had to.

We really needed this tent. So, I rolled up my sleeves. With the owner's permission, I spent the evening designing a branded invoice on their behalf. I even mocked up a temporary logo to give it credibility. I added every detail, from the tent's specifications to bank account information, so the client could pay them directly.

I didn't charge for this, and I wasn't offered any compensation. However, I wasn't simply passing along a contact; I became the vendor's brand ambassador. I persuaded my client, managed communication, prepared the invoice, resolved logistical issues as they arose and dealt with problems during setup. That's more than a favour—it's a full project delivery. Unpaid work.

I wondered how easy it would have been to make mistakes on the tent specifications or price, or slip in extra figures without the vendor knowing.

That situation made me realise that being an intermediary sometimes requires real work, and it deserves proper recognition. I've also learned to reward those who go the extra mile to secure work for my company and to provide them with clarity and professionalism to make the process easier.

Smart business owners don't only create great services; they design how those services travel.

Ensure that anyone representing you has the necessary tools to do so. This does two powerful things. It protects the integrity of your brand story, and it makes life easier for the people referring you, saving them the stress of patching together missing details.

Being represented by someone only becomes risky when you leave too many gaps for others to fill.

Equip people to speak your name confidently and ensure you remain in the conversation, even when you're not physically present.

# *Builder's Note*

### Control the Story

Referrals often bring in more work than any marketing campaign.

A single introduction, a kind word or a shared contact can open doors that your brand hasn't yet accessed. It's wise to honour the person who helped the job find you.

The key is control. Without it, you risk losing your identity, your margins and even your motivation to show up fully. Your role as a business owner is to safeguard both your financial interests and your reputation. In this context, professionalism involves handling difficult discussions about markups and commissions with firmness and strategy.

### Consider:

- Do I know exactly how my quotations appear when they reach the client?
- Am I losing jobs because of hidden costs imposed by others?
- Who am I depending on for access, and what is it costing me in terms of margins or control?
- Are my contracts clear about who can represent me and on what terms?

### Action step:

Review your last five bookings. Identify where third parties affected your pricing or negotiations. Decide on one step you'll take to protect your margins and clarify your process going forward.

Part 2 has focused on building a framework strong enough to hold your vision. What comes next is learning how to make that framework endure, scale and carry you further than you imagined. Let's step into the work of creating a business that doesn't just stand but outlasts.

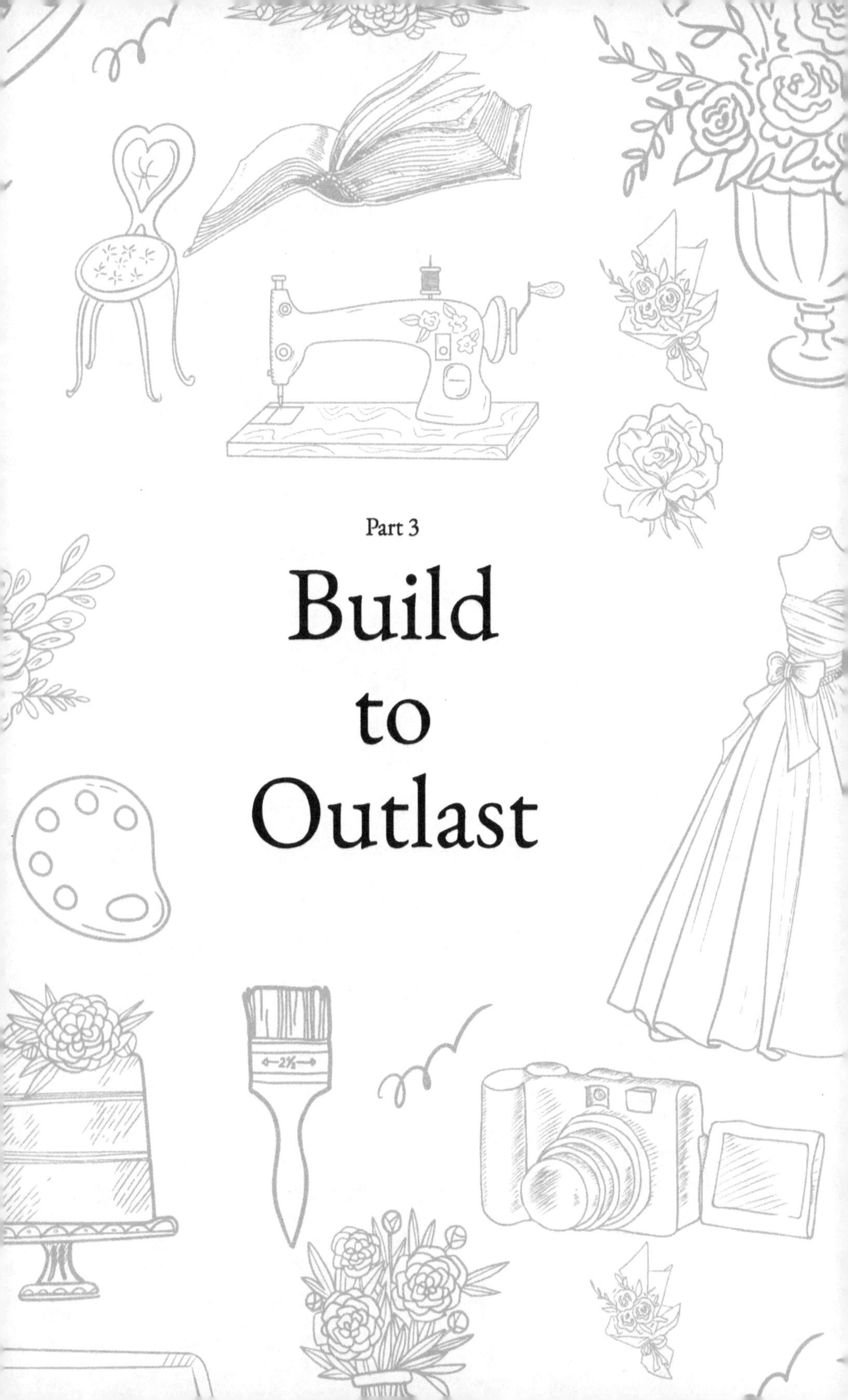



# Build to Outlast

# Chapter 14

# *Scale What Works*

**When It's Working, Work It Better**

The thrill of a new idea often feels more fulfilling than the discipline of improving an old one.

I've felt it: the urge to start afresh, to chase something different. But constant reinvention slowed my growth.

I love to create. I'm wired for novelty. Yet over time, that craving became a distraction.

It used to frustrate me when clients asked for something I'd done before. I'd present a fresh concept, full of thought and detail, and they'd scroll through my past work and say, 'We really like this one. Can we have something like it?' I'd smile and say, 'Sure', but inside, I'd shrink a little. This again?

I didn't want to repeat myself. I wanted to surprise them, and even more than that, I wanted to surprise myself. I thought repetition meant I was playing it too safe. What I didn't understand then was this: they weren't asking for the same thing. They were asking for the same effect.

That particular design—the one I kept trying to retire—wasn't my most elaborate design. But it worked. Beautifully. It was logistically sound, visually rich and easy to adapt across spaces. And no matter how many times it showed up on a mood board, clients were consistently drawn to it. I just hadn't trained myself to see that kind of consistency as success.

Creativity doesn't only live in what's new. Some of your best work isn't waiting in the next idea; it's hiding in something you've already done but haven't fully explored. And when you're wired to chase excitement, you can miss what's right in front of you.

A common mistake for entrepreneurs is thinking growth always means innovation. That unless you're launching, pivoting or reinventing, you're being stagnant. But some of the strongest businesses aren't built on constant change. They're built on doing what works again, only better.

Think about it. What if the 'next level' of your business simply requires you to take the win you already have and scale it with more intention, more polish and more profit?

Start by asking the right questions:

What's been your most effortless win lately? What design, offer or process has brought the most peace, profit or praise? What do clients keep coming back for, even when you've moved on?

That's your framework right there.

The best entrepreneurs I know don't only build, they notice. They track what's working, document what's smooth, package what's proven. They don't drop what works because they're bored. They mine it for more. They understand that depth can also be as creative as novelty.

When you do something well consistently, you become trusted. You become known. That's how signature offers are built. That's how artful businesses grow from interesting to iconic: not through constant reinvention, but through brave refinement.

So the next time a client asks for something you've done before, pause before dismissing it. That request might be pointing you towards your most scalable idea, and that's where systemising becomes crucial.

## Systemise What's Working

What feels old to you is gold to someone else.

Most clients don't care that you've created it before; they care that it was beautiful, reliable and stress-free. If it works, the real opportunity isn't in running from it but in refining it.

This shift in mindset brings clarity, but it also exposes a gap in many creative businesses: you create something brilliant, but you don't build a way to repeat it. When bookings roll in for similar work, it becomes obvious that you haven't put your house in order. You're starting afresh every time. Digging up old decks, guessing measurements, trying to remember what worked last time. Recognise this?

Creatives usually don't lack ideas; we just often forget to build anchors around the ones that work.

Real business growth comes from repetition with intention. From taking one win and asking, 'How do we recreate this with less stress, better speed and stronger execution?'

Treat every successful project like a prototype from now on. Break it down: What was the brief? How did you pitch it? What materials worked best? Which layouts adapted easily across different venues? What drew the most client praise? Which parts exhausted the team? By doing this, you're documenting the steps and capturing the DNA of the win for future use.

When something works, don't just celebrate it; study it. Archive the deck. Save the captions. Note the installation order. Keep clients' feedback. These details are the building blocks of future ease.

The moment you start writing down what's working, clarity doubles. You stop relying on memory. You start creating a system: operating procedures that become your onboarding documents, your design bible, your crew brief and your pricing reference. With each documented process, you move from reacting to leading.

Systemising turns silent genius into a shared process. It allows your wins to multiply and preserves your energy for what matters next.

Timing is crucial. The ideal moment to capture a system is when the idea feels fresh and the memory is sharp, not when you're under pressure. If your previous project went smoothly, now is the time to map out the process. If a layout made installation seamless, keep it for reference. If a client gushed about a particular detail, lock it in as a non-negotiable.

The business you want later will be built on the systems you create now.

And once you have a system, there's one more thing that will make it pay off: consistency.

## Consistency Is Your Best Marketing Plan

Excellence may attract clients, but consistency is what retains them.

Anyone can promise great work. Fewer can promise great work, delivered with the same high standards, every time.

Maintaining high standards might mean refining your process so the finish is cleaner or upgrading your materials so the result lasts longer. Over time, these improvements become part of your reputation.

That's what makes the difference: the repeatable excellence.

It's easy to assume clients only want 'wow' moments. But often, what they truly seek is dependability: the calmness in your communication, the timeliness of your response, the way your invoice aligns with your proposal, the steadiness of your tone even if the brief gets complicated.

These aren't dramatic gestures, but they build conviction: 'I can trust this person again'.

During one of our busiest seasons, we didn't advertise much. Yet referrals kept coming because each client received the same level of service—consistent communication, attention to detail and a thorough close-out process. That consistency did more than any advertisement ever could.

When your brand feels consistent in tone, process and delivery, it creates confidence in your business. People stop watching you with caution. They start sending others your way because they're sure you will not only show up, but show up well.

The mistake we make is thinking every sixty days requires a reinvention: a rebrand or a new style. Your audience doesn't want a new version of you every quarter. They want proof that your excellence isn't a one-time event but a standard you uphold.

This doesn't mean everything has to look the same. It means your message doesn't change with every trend. Your quality doesn't depend on your mood. Your brand doesn't seem like it's experimenting on them.

The more stable your systems are and the more committed you are to maintaining and refining that standard, the easier it is for people to remember and recommend you.

The vision is to become unmistakable, every time.

## Solid Groundwork Sets You Free

By now, you've noticed the pattern: identify what works, build a method to repeat it and deliver it consistently.

That's the groundwork. Without it, every project feels like a new mountain to climb. With it, you have a solid foundation that supports your progress.

Growth doesn't always result from cramming in more work. It often comes from creating a system to deliver the same high-quality work repeatedly without your business coming to a standstill in between.

Until you realise that, your business might seem successful from the outside but still pull you back into difficulties after each job. Projects may be closing but not compounding. The same small gaps will continue to reappear.

The way to break free from this cycle is by creating a system that can operate without you. A framework that transforms brilliance into something repeatable. The kind that ensures a good result becomes a consistent one. This is what frees you from playing the hero every time and allows you to focus on growing and safeguarding your business.

This is how legacy-minded thinkers approach growth. They don't just retire a successful idea; they preserve it. That beautifully executed job you're ready to move past? They understand that within it lies a process worth documenting and scaling.

That project you can't quite replicate? They know it points straight to the gaps in the business. The rushed voice note, the shaky handover? To a legacy builder, these are signals that it's time to establish order for the future.

Before you chase the next big thing, stabilise the last one.

Groundwork is what gives you the freedom to scale. And true scaling involves protecting what works so well that it becomes the signature your business is known for.

# *Builder's Note*

## Scale What Works

The fastest way to scale isn't to keep starting over, but to double down on what works. Give it roots deep enough to hold and wings strong enough to carry you forward.

Here's where you should begin:

- Identify your most recent win that felt profitable, peaceful or repeatable.
- Break down why it worked.
- Turn those insights into a simple process or checklist.
- Teach it to someone else.
- Repeat it—calmly, clearly and with less chaos than before.

That's how you scale: by polishing and perfecting what already works.

# Chapter 15

# *Build Wealth, Not Just Revenue*

## Dirty December

In Nigeria, December is more than just a month. It's a marketplace.

Dirty December, they call it, and with good reason. It's the season of events. A goldmine for service providers. If you're in the event business, you know what this means. That's when the floodgates open; parties everywhere, concerts daily, weddings every weekend and even midweek, brand activations squeezed into any available day. Clients offer anything to get their events prioritised. Planners panic. And vendors are overbooked and doubling prices.

For event professionals, it's the season that justifies the entire year . . . or is it?

I remember one particular December. It was our busiest ever. We had bookings back-to-back. Five major events in the first eight days, two of which required overnight setups. By the second week, we had no inventory left in the warehouse. Even our spares were out on rent.

Everyone was saying it: 'This is the best year yet'.

But when we sat down in January to review the numbers, something didn't add up. After paying overtime, rush production costs, freelancer fees, replacement costs for damaged inventory and logistics premiums, the profit margin looked . . . ordinary. Underwhelming, even.

It was hard to accept that all our efforts hadn't made us wealthier. We had moved more materials, worked longer hours and stretched every team we had, but the return didn't match the pressure. On the surface, the revenue seemed high. But so were the expenses, the risks and the stress. And for what?

That season taught me the difference between revenue growth and profit intelligence. One makes you feel successful. The other makes you sustainable.

More jobs don't always mean more money. In fact, they often expose where your systems are weak, your pricing is soft or your expenses are uncontrolled. When your calendar is full, every crack in your business model becomes more apparent.

By January, it was obvious we had chased volume, not value. The so-called 'gold season' that barely left breathing room and created exhaustion which we carried into January, wasn't paired with the financial cushion we had expected. It was painful to admit it, but all that work, all that pressure, all that sacrifice . . . wasn't worth it.

There were no bonuses that year. No margin to invest in new inventory. No financial cushion for the team. Despite how much we moved, we didn't move forward.

That changed how I looked at busy seasons. From then on, I stopped asking how many events we had booked and started asking how well each one was priced, managed and delivered.

We focused on:

- Tighter project caps—no more overbooking just to 'maximise December'
- Sharper costing—including real margins for staff health, logistics and equipment turnover
- Better client education—setting firmer timelines and expectations from the beginning
- Financial planning—ensuring one season's income lasts beyond the next month's bills

I generally stopped trying to win December and started focusing on winning the year, because being booked, busy and broke doesn't build anything sustainable.

## The Maths You Never Learned

A full calendar doesn't always mean a full account.

Most of us weren't taught the maths that truly matters in business. We know how to set our prices, make a budget and maybe even track income. But building wealth? That requires a different kind of maths—one that looks beyond simply adding revenue and subtracting costs.

I didn't learn it at school. I didn't learn it from watching others. I learnt it the hard way, through the frustration of running a thriving business that wasn't leaving much behind.

How do you begin understanding the real numbers that drive a business forward?

First, think carefully about it:

What does it *really* cost you to produce your service? Materials, time, team, transport, rentals and overhead. What is left after expenses? And even that isn't clean profit if you haven't paid yourself.

Some projects bring in more revenue but require high expenses for execution. Others may seem smaller but leave more behind after expenses.

These are some of the numbers to look out for:

- True profit margin per job.
- Your hourly worth: If a project takes 150 hours of your time, what does that translate to in earnings?
- Category of project that gives you the best returns with the least stress.
- Cost per project phase: design, preparation, execution

The maths you need involves being honest about what you are truly gaining from the work and not getting distracted by the shiny numbers on the invoice.

To improve clarity, I designed a simple spreadsheet that broke down each project's cost by stage. Every hour was accounted for, every cost weighed against the outcome. It was sobering at first, but it changed how I planned. I stopped chasing jobs that only looked big and started choosing jobs that were truly worth it. Sometimes that meant doing fewer or smaller events, but the results were more rewarding.

The maths we weren't taught is the maths that makes sense of a business: the true numbers that prove whether our work is building wealth or simply keeping us busy.

## The Owner Gets Paid First

It took me longer than I'd like to admit to stop treating myself like an afterthought in my own business.

There were months I paid staff and vendors and even refunded difficult clients, yet I took nothing home. I convinced myself it was normal. That founders should make sacrifices. That the business should always come first. But I've come to believe that if the business pays everyone but you, it's not worth your time.

As creatives, we often feel more emotionally attached to the brand than the balance sheet. We justify unpaid labour with passion. We confuse growth with grind. And we assume our payday will come later—when we scale, when we increase pricing, when we land the 'right' clients. But if you don't infuse your compensation into the foundation from the beginning, there will always be something more 'urgent' than paying yourself.

I used to treat my income like a leftover. If anything remained after an event, then I could take a little. But the moment I flipped that logic and saw myself as a non-negotiable part of the cost of doing business, everything changed.

Now, I plan my projects with my income as a line item. I don't hide it. I don't shrink it. I don't apologise for it. I factor my salary into our operating budget, just as I do with other important expenses. Because my role is vital. My brain, my time and my leadership are not free. And when I'm compensated, I lead better. I stop operating from a place of resentment. I'm no longer silently counting how much I've given without receiving anything in return. I'm steady. I'm clear. I'm free.

Paying yourself is a responsibility. It compels you to run the business as a genuine company. It enhances your pricing strategy. It encourages you to consider sustainability. And, no, the initial amount may not be extraordinary, but it is symbolic. It's you saying, 'I respect my work. I value my time. I'm building a business that pays me, not one that drains me'.

The moment you stop working for free within your own company is the moment you start to build genuine wealth.

## Build First, Enjoy Later

With early success comes pressure.

At first, it feels like a reward. Finally, the bookings are consistent, the invoices are being paid and the bank balance isn't in crisis mode. You've moved beyond the survival phase and can finally breathe. You have real options now. You glance at your account balance, and for once, it feels comfortable. No panic. No calculations about whether you can cover salaries and still acquire inventory.

For a brief moment, you think: Maybe it's time to upgrade. Change the car, move into a bigger space, take that holiday you've postponed three times, approve the branding refresh, say yes to all the shiny things you've been admiring. And honestly, you deserve to enjoy it.

You've worked hard. You've earned this. But this is also the moment that distinguishes short-term income from long-term wealth.

When money first starts flowing in, your business is still fragile. One bad month, one unpaid invoice, one unexpected expense, and you're back in panic mode. That's why early wins need to be treated like seed, not harvest.

Money spent on appearance buys attention, while money invested in a foundation buys freedom.

Early spending on upgrades, lifestyle inflation or unnecessary expansion can trap you in stress instead of securing your future. This can delay genuine wealth. It also forces you to hustle harder instead of allowing your systems to multiply your peace.

In our case, once we started getting the December season right and ending the year on a high note, the following year always came with high pressure to upgrade.

'We need a bigger warehouse'.

'We should get branded trucks'.

'We need to invest in more glamorous props'.

On the surface, it sounded reasonable, but I knew the business wasn't ready. We were still one logistics error away from disaster. Still one delayed client payment away from cash flow stress. Still using human energy to hold up what should have been run by systems.

So instead of spending to impress too early, we decided to invest in strengthening the business processes. These aren't glamorous decisions, but they kept us steady when things slowed down. When other businesses contracted, we had room to consider our options. When clients delayed payments, we didn't panic. When I took a proper break, the business didn't fall apart.

That's the difference between investing in comfort and investing in capacity.

And it's a decision every entrepreneur must face.

The founders who succeed in scaling are those who make wise decisions with their money. They invest in systems, people, buffers and tools that enhance their peace of mind.

Yes, celebration will come. But if you want to enjoy without fear later, the principle is simple: Build first. Enjoy later.

## The Wealth Habits of Legacy Builders

It's all about the mindset.

Legacy builders think differently. They don't just earn differently; they relate to money in ways that reshape the entire makeup of their business. It's not because they started richer or smarter. It's because somewhere along the line, they stopped building for recognition and started building for continuity.

Legacy builders see money as a resource. To deploy, not devour. To build frameworks, not fund impulse. To buy freedom, not just comfort.

They play long games in industries obsessed with quick wins.

It's easy to assume wealth is about negotiating bigger deals, attracting high-end clients or charging premium rates. Those matter, but they're not the root.

I've seen talented business owners who consistently earn good money yet never seem to get ahead. They're working hard, but they're still thinking like earners, not owners.

The turning point comes when you stop asking, 'What do I need this month?' and start asking, 'What would make this business thrive without me in five years?' That single question reframes everything.

It changes how you see a packed calendar: as a signal to automate.

It changes how you treat a great season: as seed for reinvestment.

It changes how you measure success: not by the month's balance, but by what's compounding over time.

Legacy builders resist the emotional highs and lows that keep most founders stuck. They resist the panic when the bookings slow down, the euphoria when payments land, the temptation to upgrade because 'things are looking up'. They anchor themselves in stability instead of chasing adrenaline.

I've learnt that wealth is a pattern. It's the confidence built on habits that endure—whether or not the bookings are exciting, whether or not you're being celebrated. It's the patience to let your work speak over time. The restraint to delay some things for the sake of greater purposes. The maturity to accept that you can't be invested in looking rich and actually building wealth at the same time.

If you want to build a business that supports you, not one that drains you, you must rewire how you respond to opportunities, pressure and progress.

Legacy builders operate differently. They listen for what's sustainable. They ask tough questions even when things are going well. They let the chase for attention pass them by because they're aiming for impact that lasts.

It shows in their numbers and in their stance. You'll notice it. A calm business. A steady business. A business life that's rooted, not reactive.

That's the wealth worth building. That's the posture we should protect.

# *Builder's Note*

## Build Wealth

Legacy builders understand something most people miss: true wealth isn't measured by what comes in, but by what stays and multiplies.

It's easy to measure success by revenue, by how full the calendar looks or by how much has arrived in the account this month, but those numbers alone do not tell the whole story.

Pause and reflect:

- How much of what comes in is actually staying, multiplying and securing tomorrow?
- Will this season's wins still matter in five years, or will they fade once the rush is over?

True wealth grows when money is treated as a resource to be managed, directed and protected. It is built on steady decisions that create margin and continuity.

# Chapter 16

# *The Team Is a Mirror*

**Would You Work for You?**

Your gift created the brand. Your leadership will determine if it lasts.

If your business put up a job listing, would you apply?

Imagine reading this:

An unprofessional brand seeks a team member to work weekends, follow vague instructions, operate without a set timeline, receive feedback only when something goes wrong and thrive in constant change. No onboarding. No growth plan. Must read minds. Salary: Emotional exhaustion and one random 'thank you' every two months.

Now tell me, would you take that job? Because some of us are asking people to do just that, to work under vague expectations and shifting boundaries.

There's a difference between being a brilliant talent and being a fair leader. Your team may admire your vision, your excellence, your originality. But they might also be exhausted, because working for someone gifted but inconsistent is confusing.

This doesn't mean you're a bad boss. You may simply be a former one-man show learning how to build something bigger than yourself. That requires a different skill set, one that doesn't rely solely on creativity.

I used to expect my team to just 'get it'. I thought because I could see the full picture, they should too. But they weren't inside my brain. And I wasn't giving them anything solid to work with, just scattered feedback, inconsistent involvement and stress.

It took one honest team conversation for me to understand that they weren't lacking talent. They were confused because I was running the business on impulse.

And the worst part? I thought I was the organised one.

Awareness changed everything. I learned to stop expecting loyalty without good leadership. Your team isn't only there to help you meet deadlines. They're building something with you. Whether they stay, grow or start hiding in the background depends on how well you lead, not how well you design or deliver.

So ask yourself honestly: Would you work for you? Would you trust you? Would you feel safe to grow under your leadership? If the answer is shaky, don't panic. But do make adjustments.

Great work gets attention. Great leadership keeps it.

If you wouldn't work for you, why should anyone else?

**Fighting the Mirror**

Isoken—my partner, my problem. Or was she?

A few years after Dezua started, my sister Isoken quit her 9–5 job to join me officially on this journey. She was supportive from the very beginning. Too supportive sometimes, if I'm being honest. I had the ideas, the drive and the vision, and she believed in them. She believed in me.

She had this calm, gentle loyalty that never wavered. She held the frontlines—client communications, vendor follow-ups, chasing balances, keeping things moving—while I designed and built the brand. And I loved her for it. But over time, it didn't feel equal.

I was the one staying up all night before event days. I was the one leading the team onsite. I was the one designing props for fabrication, editing designs, talking to vendors and keeping every moving part in motion, and I also held the frontlines with her. I managed most of the client communications, late-night calls, clarifications and fire drills. The emotional work. The panic work.

Somewhere in my mind, that meant I was doing double—her job and mine.

And maybe that's where the resentment began to brew. I judged her calm. Mistook it for laziness. Compared her rhythm to my chaos. And every time I took a hit from a client or the team dropped the ball, it felt like I was alone on the battlefield.

She could travel, rest or go silent for a week and nobody pursued her. But if I dared to disappear for 48 hours, the entire operation shook. It felt unfair. At least, that's what I told myself.

So I fought her.

We had SMS battles, which were mostly me typing long messages with a steaming head and her replying with calm one-liners that made my chest burn.

During one of those typical text wars where I unleashed my 100-word essay, she said something in her usual one-sentence wisdom that made me think.

'You say you're handling too much, but you don't delegate'.

I wanted to argue. I wanted to be right. But deep down, I knew she was telling the truth.

She carried on, 'You complain about doing everything, but you don't actually hand anything over. You don't think we can do it like you do, so what do you expect?'

I hated how accurate that was, but she was right.

Isoken had been doing her part. A different part. A calmer part. But a necessary one. And my own refusal to let go was part of the burden I continued to bear.

I had to ask myself a sincere question: Was she truly the problem, or was I simply afraid to relinquish control?

The control I believed made me responsible was gradually making me resentful. The support I claimed I lacked was already by my side; I just didn't know how to utilise it. She wasn't the one failing to show up. I was the one refusing to allow someone else to take the spotlight with me.

Reflecting now, I realise the gift God gave me in Isoken. Her calmness kept the business steady when I was overwhelmed. However, because her approach didn't resemble mine, I dismissed it. I wanted her to burn out like I was, to prove she was equally committed.

Sometimes, leadership involves learning to receive the help you claim to want, even if it doesn't look the way you expect.

Isoken has always been the voice of reason in my head. And our differences show up clearly in the way we handle situations in the business.

A good example of this was the day I walked away from event planning. A client asked why my hostesses were 'so expensive' and if their fee 'covered following his guests home'.

The disrespect!

I shut it down on the spot.

The insolence!

I didn't give him the chance to explain or play it off as a joke. I was done. That was it for me. I pulled out of the event and stopped offering planning services altogether. I was already overwhelmed with the weight of offering both design and planning services anyway.

Isoken would have handled that differently. She's calmer. Less reactive.

I'm the one who always wants to refund a client at the first hint of disrespect in their tone or discomfort from their behaviour. Having a partner who's more patient keeps me grounded. She helps me pause, see the bigger picture and focus on the long-term growth of the business instead of reacting in the moment.

Looking back, I now see that the partnership has been one of Dezua's greatest strengths. We don't work the same way, and that's exactly why it works. Where I'm quick to react, she's measured. Where I push for bold moves, she brings balance. Her steady presence allows me to lead without burning the business down in the process.

Strong businesses are rarely built in isolation. The right partnership is a force multiplier. You don't need someone who works exactly like you, but someone whose strengths complement yours. That might be a co-founder or director with a different temperament, a brand collaboration that opens doors, a supplier who guarantees consistency or a service partner who keeps things running smoothly behind the scenes.

Growth occurs when you create a network of strengths that takes the vision further than you could alone. So, the real question is: Who's sitting at your table?

## The Bottleneck Was Me

Two hours had passed since I'd asked Chioma for the invoice.

A task that would've taken me ten minutes. I was pacing, annoyed, trying to resist the urge to just do it myself.

I picked up my phone and called, 'Chioma, I'm still waiting for the invoice. Why is it taking so long?' She replied politely that she was still working on it.

In that moment, I assumed she was being slow. Only that, she wasn't. She had other deliverables on her plate. And likely, she didn't think the invoice was a priority. Why would she? I hadn't said it was. I hadn't defined what urgent meant. I hadn't created a system where priority was obvious.

She was responding to the culture I had built: a culture where clarity only existed when I was there to give it. That invoice delay was a symptom. The real issue was underneath. I had hired a team, but I hadn't trained them into the exact framework I now desired.

My team didn't lack talent. They lacked context.

That moment with Chioma wasn't just about her pace; it was about my lack of communication. I hadn't been clear about what I wanted, and I knew I couldn't keep leading that way if I wanted an efficient team.

So I started retraining myself.

Instead of asking, 'Why didn't they do it faster?' I started asking, 'What didn't I make clear?'

Instead of stepping in to rescue projects, I stepped back and built the kind of tools that would prevent the panic in the first place.

I noticed that the more clarity I provided, the less I was needed. The less I was needed, the more the team stretched themselves. And the more they stretched, the more I realised what I had been holding them back from becoming.

Leadership isn't about having all the answers. It's about cultivating a culture where your team learns to discover them, whether you are there or not. Such leadership requires a different kind of energy, one rooted in trusting the people you've employed and providing them with the tools to think independently. If I had kept jumping in every time something moved slower than I liked, I would never have given my team the chance to grow.

The team was waiting for permission to take the lead. And the moment I stopped solving everything for them, they started solving things I hadn't even thought about yet.

## Hire for Who You Are Becoming

Every hire I made reflected the kind of business I had created, not the one I dreamed of.

For the longest time, I hired based on who I needed urgently, not who I needed long-term. People who could assist, not people who could take ownership. I hired for convenience. And convenience has a very short shelf life.

I understand now that I was hiring people to relieve stress but not preparing them to lead. That's how I ended up with a team that was loyal and hardworking but under-equipped for the business I was growing into. They reflected my habits, not the future I was trying to build. My need for control, not my capacity for leadership. They were functioning, but not flourishing, because I had built the right business with the wrong format.

I hadn't evolved my hiring mindset to match the business I was building. I was still hiring for who I was, not who I was becoming.

The version of me I was growing into didn't just need assistance; she needed alignment. A team that could think, decide and sometimes even challenge her.

The next phase of growth demanded that I step back and ask harder questions about every new hire:

- Do they reflect where I'm going, or where I've been?
- Do they amplify what I do, or do they simply relieve what I carry?
- Are they a culture fit for the version of the business we're evolving into?
- And more importantly, am I prepared to let go enough for them to flourish?

The danger of building a team based on your present limitations is that you'll always hire small, think small and stay small. But the leader you're becoming doesn't need more task managers or followers. You need thinkers, calm problem-solvers and initiators: people who don't wait for you to figure everything out first.

Hiring for who you're becoming is uncomfortable. It tests your budget. It humbles your ego. It forces you to grow into a leader who can actually attract and retain the kind of team that builds with you. And once you taste that kind of alignment, you'll wonder why you waited so long.

Hiring well depends on energy, discernment, alignment and timing. It's recognising that your team becomes an extension of your leadership style. And if you're hiring while stuck in panic mode, you'll keep surrounding yourself with people who require managing instead of people who bring momentum.

You're no longer building for where you are. You are building for where you're going, and you need to hire accordingly.

## Build a Team That Thinks

I didn't expect much that morning.

I had to drag myself to work. I was dreading the pile-up of decisions that needed to be made. But when I arrived at the warehouse, the team had already organised the loading plan, rerouted the logistics and fixed the inventory mix-up—without me.

It caught me off guard. This didn't feel like the same team I had just a few months ago. This was a different team. They had grown. They were now efficient. For the first time, the team wasn't just carrying out instructions. They were making decisions.

It showed initiative. It showed problem-solving.

A team that only executes is limited by your capacity. But a team that thinks broadens what's possible. And to build that, you have to give people room to use their judgement.

With a thinking team, I had to change how I participated in meetings. Instead of giving answers, I began asking questions. Instead of checking every detail, I allowed the team leads to present their solutions. I stopped second-guessing what was already decided, even if I would have done it differently.

I realised that leading a thinking team is also not easy. It takes longer to develop because it involves teaching, unlearning and letting go. But when it clicks, it liberates your mind. It expands your reach. And it transforms your business from a one-person genius model to a thinking ecosystem that can operate independently.

A thinking team doesn't mean everyone becomes the CEO. It means everyone starts owning their space; bringing solutions, asking better questions and understanding how their role connects to the bigger picture.

That's the sort of team that builds with you. A team that considers the work even when you step back.

**Give Them a Vision**

Your team reflects your energy.

They're always reading the cues. The way you show up sets the tone for how others show up.

You can delegate tasks, assign roles and set up systems, but without vision, they will struggle to perform at their best. They won't feel connected to a deeper purpose. And when purpose is missing, excellence becomes optional.

Vision is how you present the future to your team in a way that motivates them to help build it. It's a steady reminder of why the work is important and its direction.

When your team understands the vision, they start thinking with you, not just executing for you.

- They begin making decisions that align with your values.
- They challenge weak ideas, even yours.
- They anticipate what's needed instead of waiting for your instructions.
- They start thinking like partners.

This kind of culture is built intentionally. It's built when you take time to show the big picture, not just in slides or plans, but in conversation and consistency. It's built when you let them hear your thought process, not just your commands. It's built when you stop hoarding the strategy and start mentoring them into it.

If your team is unsure of what matters most, it may be because you haven't shown them your priorities.

The absence of vision leaves room for something else: fear, confusion, ego or indifference. Without vision, people default to their own priorities, and rarely the right ones.

A team without vision may still be functional, but they won't be powerful. They'll work. They'll deliver. But they won't grow the business with you, because they've not bought into the future you're trying to create.

Sharing the vision isn't a one-off event. It's a rhythm. It needs to be heard in how you give feedback, how you correct mistakes and how you celebrate wins. It should be echoed in your decision-making, in what you reward and what you're willing to walk away from.

You can't build a visionary team with reactive leadership. You build it by being steady. By casting the vision so clearly and so often that they don't just hear it, but start to see themselves inside it.

When your team believes in the future you're building, their posture changes. They stop asking, 'What do you need me to do?' and start asking, 'What's the best way to move us forward?' That's when your business begins to outgrow your capacity. And not in a scary way. In a good way. In a finally-it's-not-just-me kind of way.

Vision empowers your team and frees you. Because when they can see it, they can carry it.

# *Builder's Note*

## Build Builders

Your team is a mirror. They reflect the coherence or confusion of your leadership, the tone you set in a room and the systems (or lack of systems) you've created.

You may not realise how long you've been stuck in roles that no longer suit you. It's easier to blame your team's hesitation or mistakes without asking the difficult question: Have I truly empowered them to think, decide and lead?

This chapter was about becoming more aware, seeing clearly and choosing better responses, even when it's uncomfortable.

So pause here for a moment. If someone were to shadow you for a week, what would they see?

- Would they see clarity, or confusion?
- Would they see a leader who empowers, or one who over-functions?
- Would they feel safe to grow under your leadership, or shrink around it?

You're now cultivating a leadership culture that can grow, endure and even surpass you. Your team observes more than just your instructions—they observe your standards.

Sometimes, the only upgrade your business requires is elevating the standards of what and whom you accept.

Let's keep building, with less weight, more wisdom and a team that reflects your next level.

Let's build builders.

# Chapter 17

# *Chief Energy Officer*

## The Calm Is the Real Skill

'No matter what we are going through, this event must end tomorrow'.

My manager, Sam, once said those words to me during a hectic wedding setup, and they have never left me. Over the years, I've reworded them into a personal mantra: 'Every project must come to an end'. Those words have saved me more times than I can count, especially on days when stress threatened to take over.

One of those days came when I thought I had moved past the burnout phase. The setup day arrived, and the chaos caught me once again.

The brief was sent early. The floor plan was approved. The mood board was circulated. Preparations had begun days in advance. I even walked through the design with each department lead. And yet, on the day of the event, it felt like no one knew what they were doing. Calls came every two minutes. Messages asking for confirmation I had already given. Managers who had been part of every discussion suddenly appeared confused.

At some point, it stopped being frustrating and started to feel personal. Why were they waiting for me to validate every move?

I lost my temper. And when I felt myself nearing the edge of a meltdown, I did what I always do in moments like that: I stopped answering the phone, put my device on DND and took an overdue nap.

What began as my coping mechanism became something else entirely. The silence gave me space. It cleared my head. It reminded me of Sam's words—this project, too, would surely come to an end. And for the first time, I chose not to fight, not to rescue, not to hover. I let them handle the rest of the event without me, because at that moment, I cared more about my sanity and energy.

I expected disaster. I was mentally prepared for it. What I got instead was a completed setup, a satisfied client and a team that surpassed my expectations.

I had stepped back in frustration, and I realised that what I found was far more valuable than a teachable moment. I finally understood what it meant to protect my peace, and the business survived.

From then on, I started aiming for calm.

Calm is a discipline. It's a leadership choice. A skill worth developing.

The most effective version of me no longer jumps at every ping. She doesn't over-explain, over-manage or overthink. She listens. She observes. She maintains the balance. That steadiness benefits my business more.

Calm isn't the absence of problems; it's the presence of perspective. It's the state that allows you to lead when nothing is in your control. And legacy-minded leadership learns to value that state because it sustains more than projects; it sustains the builder.

So now, I make decisions from that stance, intentionally. And I'm building systems to support that rhythm. Because the real work of a leader is to shape an organisation that can thrive without constant withdrawals of your energy.

Leadership outlives panic when you choose calm. And businesses outlast their founders when leaders build from a place of composure.

## Fire Yourself from the Wrong Roles

Calm helped me see what panic used to blur.

I could see clearly that some of the roles I was still holding onto no longer fit. I had simply been clinging to them out of habit. Hovering, double-checking, pre-empting mistakes I hadn't even given anyone the chance to make.

That clarity made it impossible to keep ignoring how much weight I was still carrying. The calls I still answered. The tasks I kept circling around. The roles I'd outgrown but never let go of.

Sometimes what appears to be deep commitment in leadership is actually just anxiety. You double-check, over-confirm and insert yourself into areas where you don't need to be. You act as if your presence is vital because you haven't learned to trust what happens when you're not there.

I stayed in that space for far too long, convincing myself I was being responsible, when in reality I was over-functioning.

So, I stepped back.

It wasn't strategy that made me step back; it was mostly exhaustion. I had nothing left to give. Yet, when I removed myself from the chaos, the business kept moving. The result wasn't perfect, but the execution still worked. The team stepped up. The clients didn't notice a thing. In fact, they had a great experience. The outcome didn't suffer, and I didn't need to rescue anyone.

For the first time, I wasn't frustrated by what was missed; I was fascinated that it had worked without me.

I decided to experiment some more. What if I stayed in the background a little longer? What if I let the framework I'd built carry the team, instead of rushing in to fill the gaps?

The shift didn't happen all at once. But I started letting go gradually. I stopped offering solutions before someone asked. I stopped assuming a task was mine simply because I knew how to do it. Little by little, I removed myself from roles that didn't need me, because I needed to create space for the kind of leader I was becoming: the kind of leader who could think clearly and guide effectively.

The moment I let go, my nervous system relaxed. The tension

eased. The urgency faded away. I finally experienced what it meant to feel supported—by people and by the processes I had spent years developing. The business was running smoothly, and it started to hold me together as well.

I began asking more insightful questions:

- Is this truly my role, or just one I never handed off?
- Does my input bring understanding, or am I disrupting a process that's already working?
- What would I do with the energy I could reclaim by stepping away?

The answers shaped me into a different kind of leader. One who wasn't everywhere but was deeply present where it mattered.

Letting go of the wrong roles allowed me to embrace those that last: the roles of vision, direction and stewardship. It restored my peace of mind and gave my team room to grow.

Because the more you release what no longer belongs to you, the more you can create a business that can outlive you.

## When What You Built No Longer Fits

The version of Dezua I created many years ago was built for a different season.

It was born out of hunger, to prove I could do this, to build something real, to show that talent and tenacity were enough. And in that season, it worked. It paid the bills. It gave me identity. It anchored my ambitions.

But over time, things changed.

I kept refining my calendar, tightening my systems and delegating more effectively. I tried all the usual ways to protect my energy. Still, the fatigue persisted.

The signals were subtle at first, easy to dismiss as a busy period. But eventually, I had to be honest. This wasn't just about stress or workload.

The business no longer fit.

And maybe, just maybe, it no longer deserved the energy I was giving it.

We don't like to admit that. Especially when it's something we built from the ground up. We cling to it because it worked once. Because it was the dream once. But sometimes, the weight we feel isn't from how much we're carrying, but from carrying what no longer aligns with who we've become.

I started noticing it in my reactions. Projects that should have excited me felt heavy. Clients I once pursued no longer aligned with my values. Even on the good days, I felt detached from the work. We were still doing well, but it wasn't where I wanted to remain.

That was the signal.

A signal that the model needed to evolve. That certain services may have run their course. That part of the business was designed by a previous version of myself who hadn't yet become this one.

It's tempting in those moments to keep fixing: adjust the workflow, rewrite the team roles, optimise, restructure, delegate. But what if the real solution isn't to tweak, but to transition? What if the best thing you can do for your future is to let go of what no longer aligns with your momentum?

This doesn't mean abandoning your business. It means it might be time to review the version you're running and ask yourself what still fits and what has gradually become outdated while you weren't looking.

Some things simply aren't yours to carry any longer because you've changed. You've grown. And now, your business needs to keep pace with your growth.

So I started asking the harder questions:

- What am I still supporting with my presence even though it no longer motivates me?

- Which parts of my current model feel heavy regardless of how rested I am?

- And which version of this business would honour who I've become?

Clarity sometimes comes from letting go, and legacy is created when you're willing to evolve what you built, so it grows to hold your future.

**Build What Builds You**

One weekend during my final year at university, I went home just to cry.

I was overwhelmed. I was the only student in my department without a project partner, and the workload for that project was heavy. I was exhausted: mentally, emotionally and physically. That weekend, I didn't want to work. I didn't want to read. I just wanted to . . . cry.

In that quiet moment, I noticed my old high school diary beneath some books on the bedside cabinet. It was a small olive-green book, filled with childish handwriting, doodles and dreams.

One entry caught my eye: I had written about opening a school someday. I had even sketched the uniforms. The name was already decided—Marigate High.

Reading those pages felt like time travel. But what surprised me most wasn't the dream itself; it was the audacity I had at that age.

So I decided to expand on it that day, giving it steps. A school seemed too distant for a 23-year-old. How about starting with something smaller, I thought, maybe a skill. I already knew I was fascinated by decorative lighting and event aesthetics.

So I wrote out this plan:

1. Become a venue designer.
2. Build an event centre.
3. Build a school.
4. Dominate the world.

It was simple and wildly ambitious. But it provided me with a starting point. I couldn't open a school immediately, but I could take the first step. That's how I arrived here. However, somewhere along the way, I forgot the rest of the plan.

In this current season of calm, I've started remembering. Not just what I wanted then, but what I want now. For too long, I got consumed by step 1. I let myself believe that because the first dream was working, I didn't need to evolve. But what if that dream has served its purpose? What if I'm allowed to create something new?

I'm not walking away from what I've built. I'm only choosing to operate from a calmer, more curious space. I'm giving myself permission to revisit the other parts of me. The parts that want to teach, to write, to create new frameworks. Maybe even to become the founder of Marigate High someday.

That little green diary held old dreams for me, but it also held reminders that I could chase new ones.

This leaves us with questions every builder eventually has to face: Is the business I'm building today still aligned with who I have become? Is it shaping me into the person I want to grow into?

It's easy to keep investing in a structure that once made sense without stopping to ask if it still does. Be honest about what no longer fits. It isn't failure to evolve, and it isn't disloyalty to rebuild. Sometimes, the most powerful step forward is to design a version of your business that suits the version of you today.

Because at the end of the day, it's about building in a way that strengthens you as much as it strengthens the business.

# *Builder's Note*

Let Go

Let go of the roles, routines and rhythms that drain your energy.

Ask yourself:

- Which part of this work still sustains me, and which part drains me?
- Am I holding onto a leadership style that no longer fits who I'm becoming?
- What would it look like to run this business from a state of calm, not chaos?

You were never meant to power everything. You were meant to protect the source, guide the work and build what outlives you.

# Chapter 18

# *The Gifted Mosaic*

## The Mosaic Mind

The superpower of creatives is versatility.

It's the wonder of doing many things well, not out of duty, but out of instinct.

We are not wired for one-track lives. We are a mosaic of layered gifts, each piece shaped by curiosity, refined through courage and connected by purpose.

You've probably noticed this about yourself. You sketch designs, but you also write captions that move people. You can string florals like poetry and still style an entire space like an architect.

Your mind doesn't stop at one medium. It stretches. It spills. It overflows.

Our career paths often have less to do with ability and more to do with choice. That's why you'll meet a fashion designer who's also brilliant at content creation, because both are expressions of visual storytelling. You'll find a photographer who writes with the same sensitivity she brings to her lens. A venue stylist who builds breathtaking scenes and also drafts scripts that read like short films. An event planner who instinctively knows lighting angles better than the videographer.

The world is often more comfortable with people who colour inside the lines, but our minds were made for the full canvas. Some of us were never meant to stick to just one thing.

But here's where it gets tricky.

You will, at some point, feel pressure to package yourself in a way that's easier to explain. You'll be told to 'narrow it down' so people can understand you. And, yes, there is value in clarity, but clarity doesn't mean you must amputate parts of your gift to make your brand easier to label.

The goal is to be intentional about how each part of you is expressed. To shape the way you showcase your skills without suppressing them. This is what the journey from hobbyist to creative entrepreneur demands: not shrinking your mosaic, but learning how to frame it.

It doesn't matter how many things you can do, but how well you manage them.

Sometimes, that involves building one clear business while allowing your other talents to support it. Other times, it requires managing two separate streams and knowing when to keep them apart or bring them together. And occasionally, it means keeping one passion purely for enjoyment without trying to monetise it.

You don't owe anyone a single-story narrative. You are a collection of powerful elements, beautifully crafted to work together. The creative mind doesn't always take a direct path, but it always leaves a trail of impact.

So, embrace your full expression. Own your mosaic. Frame it with intention. Show up with your full range. Because sometimes, the most powerful brand is the one that reflects your whole self, not just the part that's easiest to describe.

### When Everything Feels Like a Calling

There are seasons when every gift in your hand starts raising its voice, asking for attention, asking for expression.

You begin to wonder if this is God showing you the next step, or if this is just creative noise.

You feel summoned. Summoned to write, act, speak, create, build, style and teach, and somehow, none of them feel like optional hobbies. They all feel like purpose.

When every road feels like a calling, how do you determine which one to follow now? All your experiences, skills and passions may emerge simultaneously, but the timing may not align.

There's a difference between knowing what you're capable of and knowing what you're called to do now. It requires listening differently. Not everything that excites you is meant for this moment. And not every gift is meant to become a business.

So what do you do?

Begin by writing down everything you love and everything you're exceptional at. Sometimes clarity comes from seeing all your strengths in one place.

Then ask yourself:

- What do I feel comfortable pursuing right now?
- Which skill can I realistically cultivate with the resources I already possess?
- Which talent, if paused for a while, won't wither?

Don't sacrifice your other gifts to honour one. Trust that timing matters. The creative mind will always present options. The wise builder learns to pause, weigh them and proceed with intention.

## All for You, But Not All for Now

Having options is beneficial, but they become burdensome when you're unsure which is suitable for the current moment.

The challenge of having multiple gifts is that they can all seem like opportunities. And if you're not careful, you'll spend your days trying to turn every talent into a business and every interest into a source of income.

But not everything you're good at needs to bear the weight of enterprise. Some things are meant to be enjoyed. Some are meant to stay personal. Some will develop later when your life creates space for them. The issue isn't having range. It's trying to make every piece of the mosaic shine at the same time.

A useful way to move forward is to separate your gifts into three simple categories: Passion, Profit and Play:

- Passion fuels you. It energises you, even when there's no audience or reward.
- Profit sustains you. It fulfils a need and has the potential to support itself.
- Play is what you do simply because you can. No pressure, no performance.

Sometimes one gift ticks all three boxes, but more often, they'll fall into different parts of your week.

You can be serious about your creative work without turning every part of you into a project. You don't have to squeeze revenue out of everything you love. Some gifts are sacred because they remain untouched.

So before you attempt to 'do it all', put the spotlight on yourself and ask:

- What do I want to lead with right now?
- What do I want to keep sacred for myself?
- What can I play with, without the pressure of proving anything?

That's how you honour your whole self, without draining your energy by trying to show it all at once.

**Give Each Gift a Role**

If you're skilled at multiple things, trying to select just one might seem like dismissing the others. However, choosing a focus is a conscious decision to utilise your strengths deliberately.

The question to ask yourself is:

What role does this gift play in my life or business at the moment?

Not every talent needs to take centre stage. Some can support your work behind the scenes. Others enhance your visibility, strengthen relationships or simply make the work more enjoyable.

Here's one way to think about it:

- *Lead roles* are the talents you build your brand or business around. They're front-facing. They pay bills or shape your positioning.
- *Support roles* strengthen the lead. They help you communicate, market or deliver your main service with greater impact.
- *Private roles* are gifts you don't monetise or share publicly. They aren't less valuable, but they serve you in other personal ways.

When you assign a role to each gift, your expectations change. You stop forcing everything into a business model. You stop feeling guilty for setting one thing aside while focusing on another.

For example, you might be a designer who is also skilled in photography, public speaking and writing. Design could be your primary service (lead). Photography might enhance your portfolio (support). Speaking could help build trust and visibility (support). Writing could serve as your personal outlet for processing your thoughts or creating future content (private).

The balance may shift over time, but giving each gift a role helps you manage your energy, reduce guilt and move with clearer direction.

The real win is when your skills stop competing and start cooperating.

## Don't Apologise for the Range

People may advise you to narrow it down.

Choose one. Focus. Don't be confusing.

Critics and advisers often repeat what they were taught: that success is linear, that clarity only comes in single strokes, that multi-skilled people must be hard to place.

However, this is not a problem to fix. Your range is not a liability; it's leverage.

Yes, having range means you'll need to make wise choices about what leads. Yes, it means not every skill can take centre stage at the same time. But none of that means you have to cut parts of yourself off just to be understood faster.

Don't apologise for being good at more than one thing. Your range is the reason you'll thrive when others stall. It's what allows you to pivot without panic, contribute in multiple rooms and spot what others miss.

The key is to carry it with discipline, not shame. Use it with intention. Build a rhythm that lets each strength have its turn.

Being multi-skilled is not something to justify; it's something to take pride in. You don't owe anyone a simplified version of yourself.

## Your Mosaic Is Not a Mistake

Some people find their one thing and never look back. That's not my story.

I've always known I had range. I just didn't always know what to do with it.

I wanted to be an architect when I was growing up. I was excellent at creating structural drawings. But there was also a time I aspired to be a DJ. I loved the art of music and its energy, the way you could command a room without uttering a word. I also enjoyed mixing cocktails, so I was confident I'd become a mixologist. Makeup? I loved the art behind it, too, especially the colour combinations and the ability to highlight features. Videography? I can edit videos late into the night without feeling tired. Caption creation? Those strange, bizarre one-liners? They come to me effortlessly.

And did I forget to mention that I can design anything—events, clothes, homes, apps, flyers and even websites? If I had to design a machine from scratch and had the proper training, I genuinely believe I'd enjoy that as well.

I don't share all this for recognition. I say it because, for years, I believed it meant there was something wrong with me. It felt like I was trying to juggle too many things at once and not doing any of them properly.

There were seasons I'd get so good at one thing, I'd wonder if I should pivot completely. Other times, I'd watch people who had 'one lane' and envy how clear their path seemed.

However, I've come to understand that the way I'm wired isn't a glitch. I wasn't built to colour inside one box. I was built for layers. The more I embraced that, the more peace I found. I stopped explaining why I wasn't 'just' one thing. I started creating room for each part of me to matter, even if it didn't all make sense at once.

Your different gifts may not look like they belong in the same room. But they all belong in you.

This mosaic of mine? It took time to love it. But now that I do, I wouldn't trade it for anything else.

## Beau Monde

You know the saying, 'Show me your friends, and I'll show you who you are'. When I look back, I realise just how true that is. So much of who I've become has been shaped by the people I walked alongside as I tried to find my way.

In secondary school, one random afternoon, my group of friends decided we needed a name for our group. Out of nowhere, someone suggested 'Beau Monde'. I hadn't even heard the phrase before. It's French for 'a fashionable society'. The kind of stylish, sharp-minded crowd who seemed to belong in glossy magazines. But for us, it represented something more meaningful. Every letter in Beau Monde matched either the first name or surname of someone in our group. It was clever and creative, a perfect reflection of who we were.

Thinking back, that showed that even as teenagers, we were already wired to think differently.

We were endlessly curious. We loved exploring new things. We had creative minds.

We were a brilliant mix of personalities. Some could command an entire room with a single eloquent sentence, some seemed to be collecting medals and trophies and some had a natural flair for style.

But beyond all those talents, the real magic was how safe we felt with one another. In that circle, we granted each other permission to dream aloud, to share our thoughts and to try new things without fear of ridicule. We supported each other's ambitions.

Being part of that group felt like exhaling, a space where we were appreciated for exactly who we were.

That circle taught me early what the right environment can do for your gifts: it makes them braver, bolder, more visible.

It's worth asking yourself: Are the people around me helping me grow or holding me back? Do they respect my differences and my choices? Do I feel energised and inspired after spending time with them? Or do I feel like I have to shrink a little to keep things comfortable?

The right people don't project their fears onto your dreams. They let you be vibrant, unique, even a little controversial, and they cheer you on as you add new colours to your mosaic.

Life eventually moved us into new seasons, new cities and new dreams. Although the Beau Monde girls and I are now scattered across the world, the imprint of those friendships is undeniable. They gave me the courage to embrace my range.

As I continue to grow, I'm committed to building relationships that do the same, connections that add fresh tiles to my mosaic while leaving room for theirs too. Because talent may feel like a solo journey, but it rarely thrives in isolation. Talents grow in the company of people who see you fully and still urge you to go further.

Your mosaic deserves to shine brightly. And the right circle will help keep it luminous, just as it was meant to be.

# *Builder's Note*

### Let Your Mosaic Shine

Maybe you've spent years trying to tidy up your brilliance. Maybe you've been told to pick one path, as if that's what makes you serious, stable or smart.

But what if you were never meant to split yourself to be taken seriously? What if this wide, complex, colourful thing was always the assignment?

Why should you follow a neat little map when you were made to create many things in many ways?

### Consider:

- Which of my talents have I been hiding because I'm afraid of appearing unfocused?
- What patterns connect my different creative instincts?
- Where has my range achieved breakthroughs others haven't recognised?
- Am I allowing myself seasons to explore, or forcing myself into one identity?

Here's how to give your mosaic space without letting it overwhelm you:

- Capture ideas, but don't chase all of them at once. Write them down, park them and revisit them when your main work allows.
- Build clear priorities each week, so your energy knows where to land.
- Give your curiosity a home: a notebook, a digital file or a trusted person to talk ideas through with.

- Learn to tell the difference between a fleeting thought and the kind worth rearranging your life for.

Sometimes, your mosaic will be misunderstood. Other times, you'll be deeply admired. But above all, you must be at peace with the way you were made.

Your mosaic is yours alone to build. Let each piece take its place and let the whole masterpiece shine.

# Chapter 19

# *Pass on the Knowledge*

## The Work Shouldn't Die with You

If your work disappears with you, the world loses more than your talent. It loses the shortcuts you uncovered, the wisdom gained through trial and error, and the proof that building something extraordinary was possible in the first place.

Too many brilliant people keep their entire craft locked away in their heads, convinced that it's what makes them irreplaceable. And perhaps, for a time, it does. But it also traps their brilliance within the walls of a single lifetime.

Withholding your knowledge doesn't always increase your worth. It makes your legacy fragile, one unexpected turn away from collapse.

I remember a conversation that stopped me in my tracks: 'You know you've been training your competition, right? You are your own problem.'

We laughed about it, but I won't pretend it didn't sting, because deep down, I'd wondered the same. Was I giving away too much? Was I planting seeds that would one day grow into rivals?

Currently, there are far too few genuine programmes for acquiring creative skills around the world. Some of those that do exist feel more like elaborate extortion schemes than real education. High fees, recycled content, no real craft.

For a while, I struggled to understand why people are so afraid to share what they know. I've come to the conclusion that it's the fear of creating competition. Fear of losing an edge. Fear that someone else will take what they've built and run further with it.

But here's what I realised: there's an ocean of projects happening all over the world. I couldn't possibly handle them all, not in one city, not in one lifetime. If the lessons I've learned, the systems I've developed or the way I see design can help someone else build their business, serve clients better or avoid the mistakes I once made, why should that be a threat?

Sharing doesn't diminish what you know. It amplifies it. It allows your influence to reach places your feet may never tread.

Your work shouldn't die with you. It deserves to keep breathing, growing and changing lives, even when you step away.

## From Secrets to Systems

When I teach, it's never only about ideas. I go deeper.

Teaching the craft involves both theory and practical work: every technique, material and small adjustment that transforms a simple arrangement into something stunning. I don't believe in leaving people guessing. I show them the tools. I let them try it themselves. I correct them as they progress and encourage them to explore new techniques.

Over time, I've learned that even the most complex creative skills can be broken down into teachable art. A stunning floral arrangement involves mechanics, ratios, wiring techniques, foam placement and how fresh flowers drink water. Stage design involves weight calculations, structural anchoring and knowing which materials bend without breaking. Teaching these things involves turning what's instinctive for me into a system that others can follow.

Initially, that idea felt impossible because creativity often lives in tiny, invisible decisions. But I decided that if I wanted my craft to last beyond me, I needed to find language for those small decisions.

I began jotting things down: lists of materials I use and questions I always ask myself while I work. Why am I selecting this colour over that one? Why do I adjust heights in odd numbers rather than even? Why do certain flowers never approach the edge of a design? The answers became the foundation.

When I train someone now, I don't simply say, 'Place the props here'. I explain why certain props belong in certain zones. Why symmetry can sometimes kill the magic. Why certain installations require hidden wiring.

That's how you turn a craft into a teachable system: by explaining the principles and reasons behind your decisions so someone else can create something beautiful with their own expressions and interpretations.

I believe in passing on the craft because I believe there's enough business to go around. Enough events. Enough clients. Enough room for more visionaries to come on board.

When you turn secrets into teachable systems, you ensure your gift continues to create magic through others.

## Teaching Doesn't Make You Less Premium

Towards the end of my in-person training programmes, I set aside a session where my students can ask me anything. No scripts. No slides. Just an open floor and honest conversation.

I get all kinds of questions:

- How did I start?
- Where do I source my materials?
- What were my greatest mistakes?
- How do I handle difficult clients?
- What keeps me motivated when things get tough?

I answer as much as I can. I share tips, stories and the small details no one teaches in books. Then I take them into the real world. They join the team on live event setups. They see how we handle challenges on the spot, how we fix problems, how we create magic under tight deadlines.

I've been doing this for years, and I can't say my brand has suffered as a result.

Every now and then, the thoughts cross my mind:

- Am I letting people into my space too much?
- Am I giving copycats unlimited access?
- Will this make my work seem less premium?

But each time those doubts arrive, I remind myself of something deeper. I have a zeal to teach, a genuine desire to guide people who want to build something of their own. I believe there's enough room in this industry and in the world for more creativity and more voices.

Teaching doesn't cheapen your work. If anything, it showcases your true depth. It shows you're not afraid of imitation because you understand that skill alone doesn't make you exceptional. What sets you apart is your vision, your taste, your instinct and your years of experience.

When someone learns from you, that doesn't make them you. They'll bring their own style, their own ideas and their own voice to the craft.

In fact, teaching increased respect for my craft and my brand.

What makes your brand premium is mastery. And mastery is worth sharing.

## Your Wisdom Has an Audience

Sometimes your audience is close: the people you mentor directly, your staff, your industry peers. Other times, they're people you've never met or people in other industries, watching your journey from a distance, waiting for the day you decide to share more.

For a long time, I thought my skills only mattered to people in the event design industry who were seeking to launch or elevate their craft. But gradually, I discovered that my audience was wider than I'd imagined.

It started with small conversations. Someone would pull me aside after an event to ask how I manage my team or how I handle the behind-the-scenes pressure. Bit by bit, I realised that people weren't just admiring the final outcome, they were eager to understand how I think.

That curiosity grew stronger when I began offering training. I noticed how my students leaned in whenever I explained why I chose certain props or design layouts for specific projects. They weren't just interested in the finished designs; they wanted the reasoning and the practical know-how that brought the magic to life.

My audience didn't stop with the trainees either. Other creatives, event professionals and even people from completely different industries began asking me questions about business principles, staff and client management, invoicing and how to stay creative under pressure.

I started getting requests for mentorship from all over the country. It became clear to me that what I knew wasn't only useful to me; it was valuable to others.

Your wisdom always has an audience. Some people in your audience might want to follow your exact path. Others need encouragement to find their own. Either way, the lessons living in your head could be the spark they've been waiting for.

Your wisdom isn't meant to stay hidden. Not when it could save someone from a costly mistake or open doors they never knew existed. Your audience might not be a crowd filling a stadium. Sometimes it's just one person whose entire future could change because you chose to share.

That's the beauty of passing on the knowledge. It might become part of stories far greater than yours.

## Let Your Lessons Travel Further Than You Do

The moment I realised the real impact of my work and my training was when I started receiving emails and messages from people in other countries asking if I could train or mentor them remotely.

It caught me off guard. I remember reading one of those messages late at night and feeling both humbled and slightly overwhelmed. People I'd never met were asking me how to start their own businesses, how to handle clients or how to create certain designs they'd seen in photos I'd shared.

I wondered, how did they even hear about me?

I was working in my own corner of the world, focused on designing spaces, fulfilling briefs and running my business. I hadn't set out to become a voice beyond my country. But somehow, the work I'd done and the knowledge I'd shared had travelled further than my feet.

That's when I completely understood the power of letting lessons move beyond you.

Sometimes, it's a student who uses a technique you taught and creates something breathtaking halfway across the world. Other times, it's someone you've never met quietly applying your methods to their own designs. Your wisdom becomes part of someone else's journey, and sometimes you won't even know whose life you've touched.

Over time, I've learned to be more intentional about letting my lessons travel. I document my techniques more carefully. I take photos of my work in progress, not only the final beautiful shots. I record videos explaining how certain mechanics work. I save my sketches, my notes, even the random ideas scribbled on scraps of paper, because I've realised that what feels ordinary to me might be the missing piece someone else has been searching for.

Letting your lessons travel doesn't mean giving everything away for free. It means choosing which parts of your knowledge deserve to go further and shaping them so they can stand on their own.

When your knowledge travels, it often comes back to you in unexpected ways. Someone will message you, showing how they've used your technique but added their own twist. Another might share how a small tip you gave boosted their confidence. In those moments, you realise you're now building legacies.

So let your lessons travel further than you do. Because your brilliance deserves to reach corners you've never imagined.

## The Gift of Leaving a Map

A good map doesn't say, 'Go this way and only this way'.

It says, 'Here's what I've learned. Now go see what else you can discover'.

A map isn't meant to trap someone on a single road. It's meant to show them the terrain: The hills and valleys, the paths that lead somewhere beautiful, and the places where storms might gather.

That's the true gift of leaving a map. It's not about filling the world with people who replicate your every move. It's about ensuring that when you eventually step back, the wisdom you've acquired doesn't leave with you.

A map captures all of that. It holds both the victories and the warnings. It tells the next person: 'These are the shortcuts I found. These are the paths I navigated carefully. And these are the places worth the long journey'.

Over the years, I've watched people take what I've taught and transform it into beautiful creations. That honours my work, because it means the knowledge is alive; breathing, growing and evolving far beyond the limits of my own two hands.

A map isn't a cage, it's an invitation. An invitation to begin with the wisdom of those who came before and then build something entirely new. It's a way of saying: 'Here's where I began. Here's where I stumbled. Here's what I wish I'd known. But don't stop here, go further'.

The gift of leaving a map is freedom. For you, and for those who come after you. It's knowing that your mosaic of skills, stories and lessons can become the foundation for someone else's masterpiece.

And that, perhaps, is the truest form of legacy any creative can leave behind.

# *Builder's Note*

## Leave Your Map

Every time I decide to share, I discover something unexpected: respect, connection and a greater sense of purpose.

I want you to know that what you carry in your head and your hands is valuable. It's not for you alone. Someone, somewhere, is waiting for a piece of your wisdom to unlock something in them.

Don't be afraid to leave your map. Even if it feels unfinished. Even if you think no one is listening. Because passing the knowledge on means leaving lights along the path for those who'll come after you.

## Reflection moment:

- What do I know so well that I assume everyone else already knows?
- Where am I repeating myself daily that could become a training or a system?
- Who on my team could grow faster if I shared what I've learned?
- What's one part of my process I'm afraid to teach because it feels too 'mine'?
- How can teaching become part of my brand?

Identify one piece of knowledge you've been holding onto. Turn it into a document, a training session or a video this month.

Start building the legacy your business is meant to leave behind.

# Chapter 20

# *Becoming Unstoppable*

**No More Waiting to Be Crowned**

Every real builder reaches a moment when the walls they once leaned on for reassurance start to feel like cages, built by an earlier version of themselves. The one who still needed permission. The one who still needed to be noticed. The one who still waited to be chosen.

They then get to a point where they stop waiting to be crowned. They are aware that no one is coming with the perfect mic-drop validation. No one is handing out medals for restraint. No one is keeping score of how long they've waited. And the longer they keep asking for a seat at the table, the longer they'll sit outside—when they could have built their own.

It's clear to them that confidence in what they've built doesn't require outside validation. The confidence should stand firm and get the work done. That's the kind of authority they've built and earned over the years.

They've grown to recognise that they wasted so much time in the past thinking they'll finally show up big 'once things settle'. They now know the crown doesn't arrive after the next perfect client, but rests on the head of the person who knows they've outgrown waiting.

They stop tweaking, editing and hiding behind perfect planning.

They stop asking if they're enough and start owning that they've always been more than capable, but just a little too polite about it.

They acknowledge that there's no reward for humility that keeps one invisible. And nothing magical happens when they finally reach a number, hit a goal or get an approval.

This is the season they stop dimming. They are now fully aware that they've built too much to act like they are still figuring it out. There's nothing left to earn. The authority is already theirs.

They put their name on it. And claim it.

## Built to Last

You won't always be 25, or 33, or 41, or whatever age you were when the vision first took root.

The younger version of you who started this business is not the same entrepreneur running it now. And you won't be the same version of yourself steering it in another decade. That's growth. That's life. The real question is: Can the business grow with you?

It's easy to build for now. For what your calendar looks like this year. For the children at the age they currently are. For the energy you have in this season. But building a business that builds you means stepping beyond this moment and designing something that can stretch into your 40s, 50s or even 60s.

A business that respects your body as it slows down.

A business that respects your voice as it matures.

A business that matches the confidence and capacity of the legacy builder you are still becoming.

Because your business isn't just an income stream anymore. It's your educator, your wealth builder, your network expander, your mirror.

So, instead of asking, 'Is this business sustainable?' ask, 'Is this business still growing with me? Can it grow me intellectually? Is it pushing me to learn again, write again, lead better and stretch my thinking? Or has it become a routine that repeats year after year, with only my age changing?'

Can it grow you financially? Can it position you to own, invest, preserve, multiply? A well-built business grows a creative mind with multiple bank accounts, not just multiple bookings.

Can it grow you personally? Does it allow you to travel without panic? Rest without guilt? Does it give you the time to live well?

Can it still grow your voice? Does it make space for you to become a mentor, a teacher, a trainer, an author, a founder, a legacy name?

You need to decide what you're building towards. Do you want a business that looks good now, or one that ages well with you? There's a difference. You may not always want to run this version of the business. You may not always want to take on ten projects a month. But you will want income, impact, options, time, ease. So build towards that.

This is where vision becomes discipline. It's no longer about running things yourself. It's about ensuring they can run without you. It's no longer about being the star of the brand. It's about being the architect behind something that evolves, whether or not you're in the spotlight. Because the goal is to scale in a way that fits the person you'll become in five years, or in ten, or in twenty. That person might want slower days, deeper work, higher prices, more writing, less travel. She might want to mentor instead of decorate. He may want to advise rather than execute. And the business should be able to adapt to those changes, not break.

That's what it means to build to last: creating something that stretches, grows and sustains the next version of you. Because if this business can't carry you into your next decade, why are you carrying it so hard in this one?

## Protect What Pays You

Your voice, your health, your focus, your ability to think clearly and charge confidently, your name in the rooms you haven't entered yet;

all of these pay you more than you realise, but only if you protect them.

We're taught to protect the brand, the income, the deliverables. However, the real threat to a builder's future is the slow erosion of the very things that created the business in the first place: your capacity to learn, think, plan, pivot and build again.

What pays you is your ability to show up with quality again tomorrow. Your innovative engine still turning at full power. The trust your name carries. The financial margin you fought to build—and no longer need to explain. If you burn those for one more referral, one more deadline, one more 'VIP' request, you may be trading your future.

So what does protection look like when you're building for the long game?

It looks like documenting your brilliance so you can delegate it, not die with it. It looks like protecting your pricing as a sign of respect for your own process. It looks like refusing to normalise last-minute chaos, even when the money is good. It looks like reviewing your contract for coverage and capacity.

Which timelines are now too tight? Which platforms should be off-limits? What kinds of clients are now disqualified because they no longer align with the business you have worked so hard to refine?

Protection looks like shielding your calendar from urgency, your confidence from over-explaining, your voice from dilution, your legacy from erosion. Because what truly pays you is not visibility, but durability.

It's your ability to still create at 48. To still speak with strength at 55. To still design with freedom at 64. Because you built a system that didn't rob you, a standard that didn't flatten you and a brand that didn't outgrow you without you noticing. That kind of freedom is only achieved when you protect the parts of the business that make you whole, not just the parts that make you rich.

You've worked too hard to build something beautiful. Don't let your Future Self pay the price for what your Present Self refused to protect.

## Become Your Own Benchmark

Success used to be easy to measure. You could compare bookings, income, visibility and pace. It made sense back when you were trying to find your footing in an industry that felt too big. But now, you're building something custom. Something visionary. Something only you can see clearly.

At this point in your journey, comparison stops being informative and starts being harmful. Those you compare yourself with were never building what you're building.

The more unique your business becomes, the less helpful it is to look sideways. The standard is no longer, 'What are others charging?' or 'How many gigs did they book?' The real questions sound different now:

- How clearly am I executing my own ideas?
- How well does this business align with my vision?
- Is this still in line with who I'm becoming?

Because what's the point of building something successful if it no longer feels like it belongs to you?

In the earlier chapters of growth, you borrowed confidence from people who were ahead. You studied them. You mimicked a little. You stayed close to industry templates because it felt safe. But now, you're no longer growing into someone else's model. You're growing beyond it.

This is where real builders get tested. Not in their ability to grow, but in their ability to stop measuring that growth with someone else's standard. At this stage, visibility is not proof. And volume is not validation.

You could be the biggest name in the market and still not be the clearest thinker in your own company. So you need a different kind of scoreboard now. One that you can sit with at the end of the month and say:

- Our operations are more streamlined this quarter.
- Our team is thinking independently.
- Our pricing is clearer, energy is more stable and systems are holding.
- I didn't shrink, twist, over-deliver or second-guess myself at all this month.

That's what it means to benchmark your business by vision, not trends. The longer you lead, the more your definition of success must evolve. You'll stop chasing 'in demand'. You'll start designing 'in cadence'. You'll measure freedom, flow, strength of execution, ease of delegation and the maturity of your client experience. You'll stop craving to be seen and start demanding to be understood—first by yourself, and then by those who've earned access. You'll stop needing your name to be everywhere. Because you'll realise it only needs to be in the right places, at the right level, for the right purpose.

From here on, the only comparison that matters is with the builder you were yesterday and the one you're becoming tomorrow.

## Unstoppable

You didn't just build a business. You became the standard, by staying, by refining, by deciding.

Your clarity is no longer a concept. It's visible now, in your margins, your voice and the way your business runs without needing permission or noise.

What once felt like a stretch now feels like routine. The decisions that used to take days now take minutes. The boundaries that once felt awkward now sit comfortably within your onboarding process. The pricing that once made your voice tremble now flows off your tongue effortlessly.

You're no longer scaling from scratch; you're scaling from established systems. And that makes all the difference.

At this stage, the work is no longer about proving you can build. You've already built. The question now is: How far will you multiply what you've created?

You've outgrown hustle. You've moved beyond copying. You've matured beyond doubt. Now you're scaling through rhythm. Through intelligence. Through alignment. You've become a threat to everything that expected you to stay small.

The business is no longer fragile. You've moved past the stage where everything relied on your presence. You've made it transferable, teachable and scalable. Your method now exists in training decks. Your team works independently. Your vision has momentum, even when you're off the grid. Your future no longer feels like a gamble. You don't need to wonder if the next level is achievable. You've already created the model that will support it.

What began as a sketch is now a system. What felt like survival is now scale. The blueprint is effective. You've done the crucial work. You've laid the foundation. You've built the systems. You've protected the core.

You're unstoppable because you're no longer building on sand. And that—more than talent, more than visibility, more than applause—is what will carry you all the way.

The forecast is now *nine+ figures* and beyond.

# *Builder's Note*

**Beyond Building**

This final chapter is about crossing the line from builder to leader. From architect to owner. From proving yourself to protecting what you've built.

You've done the hardest part. You've sketched the ideas, built the systems and navigated through the noise. Now, your job is to stand firm in it. To let your decisions carry weight. To move with the confidence that your business exists because you made it so.

**Reflection:**

As you turn the final pages of this book, ask yourself:
- Which clients or projects no longer deserve space in my next season?
- What boundaries have I been too polite to enforce?
- How can I guard my time and health as fiercely as my profits?

**Take Action:**

Choose one hesitation and resolve it this week. Decide, announce and take action.

This is the moment to move from builder to leader. This is the season when you stop questioning if you're ready. You are. You've built the business. Now lead it.

Thank you for letting me share this journey with you. May your next season of building be bold, deliberate and entirely yours.

# *Letters to the Builder*

**Dear Newbie Builder,**

Starting out rarely feels the way you imagined. It's usually less certain. You're piecing things together with instinct, doubt and sometimes borrowed tools. And even when you get something right, it's hard to tell if it's skill or luck. Hang in there! You're not doing it wrong. This is what beginnings look like when you're building something real.

Don't worry too much about impressing people who've forgotten what the early days felt like. Learn your own patterns, make your own messes and figure out what actually works for you. Some of the best builders started exactly where you are: with questions no one answered, resources they couldn't afford and awareness that only came after trying everything else first.

The early phase is rarely smooth. You'll try things you outgrow quickly. You'll admire people whose path has nothing to do with yours. You'll feel tempted to skip ahead to the confidence, the money, the reputation. But shortcuts always cost more than they give.

Protect your enthusiasm. That energy is a resource. Sharpen your instincts. Ask better questions. Take screenshots of your wins, even if they're small. Document the messy middle. This is the footage that Future You will thank you for.

Learn deeply. Charge better, even if you're still finding your feet. Build good relationships. And take yourself seriously enough to stop shrinking when you speak. You're building an identity, one that can stand the test of time.

One day, your name will sit where you once hoped it would because you chose to keep going when it would've been easier to stop.

And you're doing better than you think.

—Mary

**Dear Evolving Builder,**

You've been at this for a while now. You've outgrown the fear of starting, but now you're burdened with the effort of continuing. You show up and deliver, yet deep inside, you're unsure how much longer you can sustain this version of yourself.

No one warns you that success can also be exhausting. The calendar fills up. The clients arrive. The work is celebrated. But amid deadlines and testimonials, you sometimes wonder if the business you've built still fits the person you're becoming. This is not a sign of weakness. It is awareness.

You're allowed to pause and ask bigger questions. Questions about the true state of your business. Questions about your mental health. Questions about your current needs.

Builder, this is your permission to evolve. You're allowed to outgrow your former brilliance. You are not obligated to keep delivering in a way that drains you.

It takes courage to restructure something that already works. But that's what legacy requires: momentum and meaning. The goal is not to stay busy. The goal is to build something that will still make sense in your next season.

Your work matters. But so does your well-being.

Keep building, but this time, build with you in mind.

—Mary

**Dear Visionary Builder,**

You've seen what others haven't. You move through life with ideas flickering like fireflies: bright, unpredictable and often misunderstood. You see beauty in fragments. You sense potential where others see chaos. And yet, the world doesn't always reward the vision.

Sometimes it's isolating. You explain your dream, and they tilt their heads. You pitch your concept, and they ask for a cheaper version. You show your work, and they scroll past it. But still, you see. And that makes you dangerous in the best way.

You're not here to blend in. You're here to create what doesn't exist yet. That means your path may feel lonely at times. Don't trade originality for applause. Protect the magnitude of your dream even when others can't see it yet. Some visions only make sense in hindsight.

Let your strategy nurture your spirit, not suffocate it. Build the kind of brand that reflects the person you're still becoming. And protect the part of you that sees in colour when others only see outlines.

Keep your eyes on the long game. Hold on to your purpose, because the world needs what only you can bring to life.

Your vision isn't too grand. It's the blueprint the future has been waiting for.

—Mary


**Dear Restless Builder,**

You're now questioning everything, but you once knew why you were doing this.

There was energy. There was excitement. You could feel the spark when an idea came alive. But now, something's different. The joy is quieter. The work feels heavier. And the clarity that once guided you like a compass is fogged over.

Maybe nothing dramatic happened. No big failure. No disaster. Just a slow, silent drift between the builder you were and the person you're becoming.

It's okay to stop and reevaluate. You don't have to burn out to justify a pivot. You're allowed to lose interest. You're allowed to want different things. Seasons shift, even for those who used to be on fire.

This moment doesn't mean you've failed; it means you're paying attention. The business may have outgrown your original dream, or you may have evolved faster than you expected. You may have built something that works, but not something you still want. That honesty is leadership.

You don't have to quit, unless quitting is what brings you peace. You don't have to force joy back into a model that no longer fits. But you do owe yourself the space to explore what else could be true.

What if you could rebuild it differently? What if the next version feels lighter? What if you loved it again, but only because you were brave enough to reimagine it?

Stay curious. Clarity waits on the other side of courage.

—Mary


**Dear Legacy Builder,**

You started with a sketch, raw, hopeful, unfinished. You didn't know exactly what to build, but something inside you couldn't ignore the call to begin.

You shaped it with insights gained under pressure. You adapted as you evolved. You built through doubt, deadlines and days that didn't always make sense. And somewhere between chaos and courage, you created something meaningful.

Now, you've seen what's possible. You've traced the missteps and watched the build take shape from sketch to system to something that can outlast one season of your life. You didn't just read a business book. You read your own potential written between the lines.

What you need, you already have: a vision, a story and the determination to keep building even when the path feels uncertain. The goal was always to become solid in who you already are and to build from that point.

Your six-figure chapter was the beginning. Your + is waiting: your next level, your next version, your next season. And when it comes, you'll know it's not luck. It's what happens when courage and creativity learn to work within structure.

This isn't just a book. It's a mirror. A blueprint. A push forward to build something worth remembering. Then teach someone else how to do it.

That's how you outlast. That's how you rise.

Let your courage guide you once more. Not just to six figures, but to becoming the kind of creative who can build beyond.

With clarity and fire.

—Mary


**P.S.** If any of these letters felt like it was written for you, good. It was.

# *Project Budget Breakdown*

No matter what type of creative work you do—whether you're producing physical products, selling digital offers or providing a premium service—your business needs a budget that reflects more than just your passion. It should mirror your process, your systems and your growth objectives.

A well-prepared budget does more than cover your costs. It helps you price correctly, make confident hiring choices, evaluate profitability and grow with purpose. It's not just a spreadsheet; it's your blueprint for long-term success.

Below is a versatile budget template. Whether you're planning a styled shoot, launching a product line, designing a backdrop, developing a course or shooting a movie, this breakdown helps you allocate wisely and price strategically.

**Sample Budget Breakdown for a $10,000 Project or Product**

| Category | Suggested % | Amount ($) | Notes |
| --- | --- | --- | --- |
| Concept Development | 2–5% | $200–$500 | Mood board, creative direction, research, strategy |
| Materials / Production Costs | 25–35% | $2,500–$3,500 | Raw materials, packaging, software licenses, content tools, decor items |

| Labour / Staff / Subcontractors | 15–25% | $1,500–$2,500 | Team pay, freelancers, assistants, contractors |
|---|---|---|---|
| Logistics / Delivery | 5–10% | $500–$1,000 | Transport, shipping, setup, storage |
| Branding / Marketing | 5–10% | $500–$1,000 | Ads, photography, influencer gifting, design |
| Admin / Business Operations | 5–10% | $500–$1,000 | Subscriptions, office/studio rent, tools, platforms |
| Contingency / Buffer | 5% | $500 | Covers last-minute changes, errors, market shifts |
| Tax | ~10% | $1,000 | Depending on location laws |
| Total Cost of Delivery | ~80% | $8,000 | The real cost to execute well and sustain the business |
| Minimum Profit | ~20% | $2,000 | Profit is not extra—it's essential. Minimum 20–40% on total cost |

## Profit Is What You Decide

Many creatives price emotionally: basing fees on 'what feels fair' or what others charge. Without a built-in profit margin, you can't run an efficient business.

Let's break it down:

- If your total delivery cost amounts to $8,000 and you charge $10,000, your profit is $2,000 (20%).
- If you charge $9,000, your profit reduces to $1,000 (10%), which may not be sufficient for reinvestment or expansion.

- If you want to build wealth and not just stay busy, aim for 20–40% profit on top of your true costs.

These percentages aren't fixed rules. Some months, your labour costs may spike. Other times, marketing might need more. The point isn't to obsess. It's to stay aware.

Even if you're not at $10,000 per project yet, think in terms of percentages. A $1,000 order follows the same breakdown. A $100 product can still yield a 30% profit if priced correctly.

The more deliberate your numbers, the less emotional your decisions.

# *The Confident Pricing Guide*

Pricing is more than just maths. It reflects identity, positioning, value and voice, all wrapped into a figure that communicates your standard.

Confident pricing doesn't begin with what the market will tolerate. It starts with what it takes to deliver well, again and again, without resentment.

## What Confident Pricing Actually Means

Confident pricing is about being unwavering when you state your rate. It's about establishing your rates on firm principles.

You should be able to:

- State your rate confidently
- Explain it without oversharing
- Charge it without second-guessing
- Walk away when it's not respected

## The 5 Layers of Confident Pricing

1. **Clarity:** Know exactly what's included in your offer, and what it costs in time, tools and energy.
2. **Margin:** Build in enough profit to grow, hire and reinvest.
3. **Positioning:** Price at the level you're stepping into.
4. **Process:** Ensure your client experience matches your rate.
5. **Conviction:** State your rate confidently, without apology or excuse.

**The Confident Pricing Formula**

True Cost of Delivery (TCoD) + Minimum 30–40% Profit Margin + Brand Value Adjustment (Premium Tier or Industry Leader Positioning) = Your Price

For example:

TCoD: $2,000 (labour, logistics, design, software) + 40% Profit ($800) + Premium Value Add ($500) = Final Price: $3,300

If you're creating high-end, white-glove or premium experiences, you can add 10–20% more to account for scarcity, expertise or access.

**Phrases to Retire**

- 'I know it's a bit pricey, but . . .'
- 'Let me know what works for your budget'.
- 'I can give you a discount if . . .'
- 'It's negotiable'.
- 'I'm still working on my rates'.
- 'It's not really about the money . . .'
- 'I don't usually charge this much, but . . .'
- 'I'm happy to tweak it to suit your budget'.
- 'I hope this is okay . . .'

These aren't just words. They're micro-permissions for people to doubt your value. And if you sound unsure, you're teaching others to question what should have been final.

**Final Notes on Pricing and Energy**

You can't demand premium while operating from panic. You can't ask for more if you've never sat down to calculate what it takes to deliver well.

Confident pricing lies in your preparation. It's about doing the work to know what you're worth and building the process to back it up. Deliver your price calmly. No apologies. No unnecessary words. That's confidence, and it's already within you.

# *Red Flags and Graceful Exits*

Every client comes with a price. Some pay in cash. Others cost you peace, profit or your reputation. You are allowed to be discerning. In fact, it's required if you want to build something that lasts.

I've created a guide that highlights the early signs of misalignment and provides the language to protect your boundaries and exit without guilt.

**Red Flags to Spot Early**

All of these are not necessary to say no. One is often enough.

1.  The 'How Much for Just . . .' Client

They want to dissect your offer and cherry-pick their own version.

▶ They don't respect your standards.

▤ Phrase to remember: 'Our process is designed as a complete experience. We don't break it down per element'.

2.  The Urgency Dancer

They need it now. They need a 'quick' version. They skip the queue and the timeline.

▶ They don't respect your bandwidth.

▤ Phrase to remember: 'Our quality requires the full timeline. We're unable to compress that without compromising delivery'.

## 3.  The Energy Checker

You feel it before they say anything. Overly demanding, unclear, controlling or simply chaotic.

⚑ If your body tightens when their name shows up, listen.

🧾 Phrase to remember: 'After review, we don't believe this is the right fit for our team'.

## 4.  The Budget Bender

They consistently push back on pricing or compare you to cheaper alternatives.

⚑ They don't respect your value.

🧾 Phrase to remember: 'Our rates reflect our experience and process, and we're unable to adjust this offer at this time'.

## 5.  The Commitment Dodger

They disappear after enquiries, delay payments, avoid contracts or stay vague about timelines.

⚑ They don't respect your boundaries.

🧾 Phrase to remember: 'We require a signed contract and deposit by [date] to confirm this slot'.

**How to Exit without Drama**

If you've already started the conversation or the project, use these clear exit lines. They are composed and calm:

- 'After further review, we do not believe this aligns with our delivery model. We wish you all the best going forward'.
- 'We won't be proceeding with this project, but thank you for considering us'.
- 'Based on our bandwidth and the scope, we'll have to step back at this stage'.
- 'This does not align with our business goals for the season'.

If you have received payment, only process refunds as your contract specifies. Use calm, neutral language and avoid sounding defensive.

*Not every opportunity is worth risking your reputation.*
*Not every inquiry warrants access.*
*Not every invoice is worth sacrificing your peace of mind.*

# *A Business Audit for Creatives*

Every business has leaks. Sometimes it's money. Sometimes it's time. Often, it's energy. You can't scale what hasn't been audited. You can't delegate what hasn't been defined. And you absolutely can't grow what's still leaking energy, profit or clarity.

This simple audit is for alignment. Use it monthly, quarterly or whenever growth feels slower than it should.

**The 5-Area Creative Business Audit**

1.  Profit Leaks

Ask:

- Am I consistently making a profit after costs, or am I just 'busy'?
- Do I know the true cost of delivering my offers?
- Am I factoring time, tools, team and margin into every price?

Action:

Audit your last three projects or product batches. Apply a minimum profit margin of 20%–40% moving forward.

2.  **Process Leaks**

Ask:

- Am I reinventing my process for every new client or offer?
- Do I have documented steps for onboarding, delivery and closure?
- Am I the bottleneck?

Action:

Systemise what repeats. Turn voice notes into standard operating procedures (SOPs). Build templates. Stop relying on memory.

## 3.  People Leaks

Ask:

- Are the people in my business helping me lead, or only adding noise?
- Is my team clear on expectations, values and workflow?
- Do I hold on to help that I've outgrown?

Action:

Reassign. Retrain. Release. Protect your culture. Lead with focus, not convenience.

## 4.  Positioning Leaks

Ask:

- Is my message clear to the clients I want to attract?
- Am I showing up like a premium brand but quoting like a beginner?
- Do my visuals and communication match the level I claim?

Action:

Tighten your website, bios and proposals. Be consistent across platforms. Speak like the version of you you're scaling into.

## 5.  Personal Energy Leaks

Ask:

- What habits, relationships, or patterns are draining me right now?
- Is my business built around my wellness, or does it consume it?
- Am I preserving my mind, body and creativity, or surviving every week

Action:

Reclaim your mornings. Build margin into your calendar. Say no faster. Protect your energy like it funds the future, because it does.

Growth arises from tightening loose areas and removing what no longer fits. Consistently fix the leaks, and your business will run more efficiently with less strain.

# *Acknowledgements*

This book may carry my name on the cover, but it rests on the strength, support and belief of many people.

To my father, late **Engr. David Onaiwu—**
You were the first person who truly believed in me. You supported my dreams, even when they didn't match your expectations for my career. An engineer deeply rooted in the oil and gas industry, you had every reason to steer me towards your path, but instead, you made space for mine. Your encouragement gave me the courage to start, and your legacy lives on in every design I create.

To my mother, **Lady Veronica Onaiwu—**
I watched you arrange flowers for the church every week and run an interior design business with grace. Your love for beauty and thoughtful spaces laid the earliest foundation for mine.

To my husband, **Nosa—**
Thank you for standing by me even when this career path didn't look like the path you once envisioned for me. For enduring the late-night calls, the stress, the obsession and the chaos that comes with building a business in Nigeria. I see you, and I'm grateful for your unwavering support.

To my children **Andrea** and **David**—

You were born into this dream and have grown with it. I hope one day you'll look back and understand what it took for me to build something meaningful against all odds. I carry you both with me in everything I do.

To my sisters—

**Esosa,** you gave me my very first taste of entrepreneurship through a holiday job in your fashion design business. That experience taught me the basics of client service and record-keeping, lessons I still apply today.

**Anthonia,** you showed me the possibility of building a business that could support a beautiful life. Even with your health challenges, you worked with unmatched strength and style. Your ambition, elegance and work ethic continue to inspire me. I carry your spirit with me in every space I design and every dream I dare to build. Rest peacefully with the angels.

**Isoken,** my baby sister and business soulmate, from childhood ideas to adult responsibilities, you've stood beside every version of me. You joined Dezua full-time when I was trying to juggle starting a family and running the business in different cities. Thank you for trusting me, tolerating me and helping me carry the vision. I will always count you as one of the greatest gifts of this journey.

To my niece, **Nadine**—

Thank you for joining me on this book journey. Your ideas and steady presence helped shape these pages in more ways than one. I couldn't have asked for a better partner in this process.

To my wonderful circle of friends, **Abas, Adesua, Akanimo, Amaka, Amara, Boma, Chizoba, Emefie, Funmi, Lily, Mudi, Nkiru, Nneka, Onyinye, Oziegbe, Tobechi, Uche**—

Thank you for being my tribe. Your presence, prayers, encouragement and love have carried me through many chapters. You've stood with me, celebrated me and reminded me of my strength.

To **Mrs Ifeyinwa Rayme Nwokah—**
Your wisdom and constant support through the years have been a true gift to me. Your encouragement has meant more than words can express. Thank you for being present in ways that truly matter.

To **Debola Lewis—**
I told you on the day I registered for your training that I would be your best student. I hope I've made you proud. Your commitment to excellence and innovation has shaped the way I approach my craft and this industry. Today, I carry that standard with me and pass it on to others.

To **The Dezua and Swanbees teams**, both past and present—
You are the hands and hearts behind every transformation. Thank you for enduring the late hours, the pressure, the shifting plans and the pursuit of excellence. You bring the vision to life again and again. I see you. I honour you.

Finally, to **every client** who trusted me, **every student** who learned from me and **everyone who believed** in this book—
Your faith turned ideas into impact, and your trust gave me the courage to keep building. You made this worth doing.
With love,
**Mary Aghedo**

# Sketch Pages

# Sketch Pages

# Sketch Pages

# Sketch Pages

# *About the Author*

· · ·

Mary Aghedo is a creative entrepreneur, an event designer and the founder of Dezua Events Limited and Swanbees Limited. With over 15 years of experience, she is known for transforming spaces with a signature blend of luxury aesthetics. Her foundation in Electrical/ Electronics Engineering and Engineering Management allows her to bring technical precision and analytical thinking to every creative project.

She transitioned from the corporate world into the creative industry, launching her business with an unwavering commitment to excellence. Today, Dezua Events is a recognised design brand serving high-end weddings, corporate activations and luxury experiences across Nigeria.

Beyond design, Mary runs an event rental company and offers hands-on training and mentorship for aspiring event professionals. Her passion is helping creatives turn raw talent into sustainable businesses.

*Sketch to Six+ Figures* is her debut book, blending memoir and manual for ambitious creatives.